Madagascar Wildlife

A VISITOR'S GUIDE

Nick Garbutt
Hilary Bradt
Derek Schuurman

Bradt Travel Guides, UK
The Globe Pequot Press Inc, USA

Second edition 2001
Reprinted with amendments May 2005
First published 1996

Bradt Travel Guides, 23 High Street, Chalfont St Peter, Bucks SL9 9QE, England
Published in the USA by The Globe Pequot Press Inc,
246 Goose Lane, PO Box 480, Guilford, Connecticut 06437-0480

British Library Cataloguing in Publication Data
A catalogue record for this book is available from the British Library

ISBN-10: 1 84162 029 7
ISBN-13: 978 1 84162 029 9

Library of Congress Cataloging-in-Publication Data
Bradt, Hilary.
Madagascar wildlife : a visitor's guide / Nick Garbutt, Hilary Bradt
and Derek Schuurman — 2nd ed.
p. cm.
Includes bibliographical references (p.).
ISBN 1 84162 029 7
1. Zoology—Madagascar. 2. National parks and reserves—Madagascar—
Guidebooks. 3. Wildlife watching—Madagascar—Guidebooks. I.
Schuurman, Derek. II. Garbutt, Nick. III. Title.
QL337.M2 B735 2001
591.9691—dc21   00-066295

Photographs
Front cover: Leaf-tailed gecko *Uroplatus fimbriatus* (Nick Garbutt)
Text Josephine Andrews (JA), Anne Axel (AA), Quentin Bloxam (QB), Deri Bowen (DB),
Hilary Bradt (HB), Marius Burger (MB), Adrian Deneys (AD), Nigel Dennis (ND),
Nick Garbutt (NG), Steve Garren (SG), Ben Gaskill (BG), Horst Gossler (HG),
Dominique Halleaux/BIOS Photo Library (DH/BIOS), Caroline Harcourt (CH),
Paul Hellyer (PH), Johan Hermans (JH), Olivier Langrand/BIOS Photo Library (OL/BIOS),
William Love (WL), Pete Morris (PM), Mark Pidgeon (MP), Frances Pirie (FP),
Brian Rogers (BR), Gavin and Val Thomson (GT)

Illustrations Nick Garbutt
Map Steve Munns

Designed by Ian Chatterton, formatted by Pepenbury Ltd
Printed and bound in Italy by Printer Trento

CONTENTS

ABOUT THIS BOOK

'**W**hat on earth is that?' asked a visitor to Madagascar as she stared at the leaf-tailed gecko in disbelief. 'Are we looking at *fulvus rufus* or *fulvus collaris?*' queried the zoologist as he observed some brown lemurs in Berenty. This book answers the questions of all visitors to Madagascar, whether holidaymakers or serious naturalists. Madagascar may lie a mere 400 kilometres off the coast of Africa, but it is separated from it by millions of years of evolution: nature's private sanctuary.

In compiling this book we have selected only the most interesting, appealing or beautiful animals, generally limiting our choice to those easily seen by visitors. And to help in the choice of places to visit, an introductory chapter describes the most accessible reserves and the key species likely to be seen there.

MADAGASCAR AND MALAGASY NAMES

The adjective 'Malagasy' is generally used in preference to 'Madagascan' by both naturalists and general writers. Malagasy is also the name of the people of Madagascar.

After independence the Malagasy were naturally anxious to replace the French colonial names of their major towns. This has posed a problem for foreigners since the Malagasy language is full of long, hard-to-pronounce names, so even the best-intentioned tour operators and visitors tend to use the old names. To avoid possible confusion we give the old names in parentheses.

ACKNOWLEDGEMENTS

The authors would like to thank the experts who generously supplied information for this book: Frank Glaw, Caroline Harcourt, Clare Hargreaves, Mike and Liz Howe, Alison Jolly, Olivier Langrand, David Lees, Angus McCrae, Gilbert Rakotoarisoa (DWCT, Madagascar), Nivo Ravelojaona, Don Reid, Ian Sinclair, Hilana Steyn and Lucienne Wilmé. Thanks also to Cathy Dean for her meticulous proof-reading in situ in Madagascar.

Many thanks also to the following photographers who did not make it on to page v: Josephine Andrews, Anne Axel, Deri Bowen, John Buchan, Nigel Dennis, Steve Garren, Olivier Langrand, Peter Morris, Mark Pidgeon, Frances Pirie and Gavin and Val Thomson; they all provided crucial images, often at the last minute. A full list of photographers' names appears on page ii; their initials appear beside their photographs.

AUTHORS AND PHOTOGRAPHERS

Nick Garbutt is a freelance zoologist with a special interest in Madagascar. He first visited the island in 1991 and has subsequently returned every year to investigate and photograph the unique fauna and flora and to lead wildlife tours. His photographs have been published in magazines and books all over the world and he has twice been a winner of the BBC Wildlife Photographer of the Year Competition. Nick is also the author of *Mammals of Madagascar* (Pica Press, 1999) and has seen 48 of the 51 lemurs in the wild.

Hilary Bradt first learned about Madagascar in 1974 when she attended an illustrated talk given by a zoologist in Cape Town. Her first visit to the island was made two years later. She has led tours there since 1982 and is the author and publisher of *Madagascar: The Bradt Travel Guide* and *Madagascar* in the World Bibliographic series published by ABC-Clio Press.

Derek Schuurman is a keen naturalist working for Rainbow Tours in London. He has written numerous articles about Madagascar. His book *Globetrotter Travel Guide to Madagascar* is published by Struik/New Holland.

Marius Burger was, for ten years, a research assistant at Eastern Cape Nature Conservation in South Africa. He leads 'herping' trips to Madagascar. His photographs have illustrated many specialist herpetological articles and books. He provided most of the *Reptiles and Frogs* chapter in the first edition of this book.

Quentin Bloxam is zoo programme director at the Durrell Wildlife Conservation Trust (Jersey Zoo) and has led numerous natural history tours to Madagascar.

Frank Glaw, who revised the *Reptiles and Frogs* chapter, is curator of herpetology in the Zoologische Staatssammlung in Munich, Germany. He is co-author of *A Field Guide to the Amphibians and Reptiles of Madagascar.*

Johan and Clare Hermans are award-winning photographers and horticulturists. They have a special interest in the orchids of Madagascar, and have completed a bibliography on the subject.

William (Bill) Love is a nature photographer, writer, lecturer and private breeder of reptiles and amphibians in Alva, Florida. His interest in everything Malagasy has led him to guiding ecotours to Madagascar and other tropical places.

Brian Rogers is a retired GP who also has an honours degree in zoology. He has had an interest in wildlife photography for many years, and his images have appeared in numerous wildlife magazines (through the agency Biofotos). He has been commended in the BBC Wildlife Photographer of the Year competition.

Madagascar pygmy kingfisher *(Ispidina madagascariensis)*

AN INTRODUCTON
TO THE WILDLIFE OF
MADAGASCAR

'Of Madagascar I can say to naturalists that it is truly their promised land. There Nature seems to have retreated into a private sanctuary to work on models other than those she has created elsewhere. At every step one encounters the most strange and marvellous forms.'

Joseph Philibert Commerson, 1771

Madagascar had been enchanting naturalists long before Charles Darwin visited another group of islands and began developing his theories on evolution. Unlike the Galápagos, which were born through volcanic eruptions, Madagascar was once part of a huge super-continent that covered most of the southern hemisphere. Some 200 million years ago (mya), when dinosaurs dominated the earth (the oldest dinosaur fossils yet discovered were found recently in southern Madagascar and date back 230 million years), Gondwanaland began to break up and the present-day continents of Africa, South America, India, Antarctica and Australia slowly moved apart.

Madagascar (with India still attached) broke free from Africa some 165 mya, and drifted southeastward. The established view is that by 80 mya Madagascar, and all the stowaway dinosaurs on it had become completely isolated. However, new fossil finds suggest that at this time it may still have been joined to India, which in turn was connected by land bridges to South America via Antarctica. This would certainly go some way to explaining the strong links that remain between present-day reptiles in South America and Madagascar.

Nonetheless it is still probable that many of the later evolving life forms we see today arrived after Madagascar had become isolated. Most likely, the ancestors of land mammals and many of the reptiles rafted across the Mozambique Channel on floating clumps of vegetation washed out to sea after heavy storms. Few survived the rigorous crossing – absent from Madagascar are many of Africa's familiar forms such as cats and dogs, along with their prey animals, antelope and other ungulates.

Geological forces thrust up the high mountain range that runs down the centre of the island, creating dramatically different climates – wet in the east, dry in the west and drier still in the south.

The flora developed according to this rainfall regime and the fauna subsequently evolved to occupy the many niches on the new mini-continent

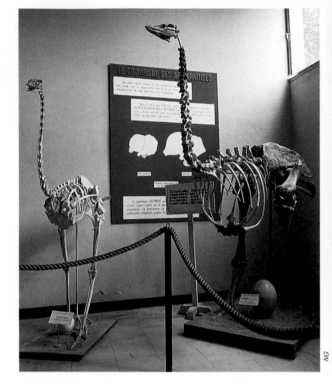

Right Skeleton of an elephant bird (*Aepyornis maximus*). This huge flightless bird, probably the largest that ever lived, is shown next to the skeleton of an ostrich. Note the massive thigh bones. It is likely that the *Aepyornis* became extinct only relatively recently, around the time of the dodo. Sub-fossil egg shells and even complete eggs can still be found in the south of Madagascar.

– rainforest, deciduous forest, rocky mountains and semi-desert. No one knows how many species there are today on Madagascar – perhaps 200,000 or more – but it is known that the majority are found nowhere else. Over 80% of the wildlife is unique to the island and much of it is startlingly different from anything seen elsewhere in the world.

Two thousand years ago an all-conquering predator arrived in this Eden: man. A thousand years later and 25 or more large animals had been wiped out, including at least 16 species of lemur (some as large as gorillas), three pygmy hippos and the largest bird that ever lived, the elephant bird (*Aepyornis maximus*). It took nearly another 1,000 years for man to recognise his folly and start protecting instead of destroying. In 1927 the French colonial government created the first reserves. Conservation took a back seat after independence in 1960 until international interest in this treasure trove of nature prompted the Malagasy government to instigate a conservation programme in the mid-1980s.

Today, Madagascar is widely considered one of the world's top conservation priorities. Many national parks and reserves are being developed for ecotourism, the nation's best chance of earning the foreign currency needed to continue its efforts to save its priceless heritage.

Evolution

Why is the wildlife of Madagascar so different? To find the answer, we need to understand the forces that create all living things: the forces of evolution.

Individuals of a species differ slightly from one another: these differences are the result of variations in their genes. Sometimes these differences convey an advantage that gives the individual a better chance of survival: that is to say improves its 'fitness'. It follows that such individuals are more likely to breed and, crucially, pass the beneficial genes to their offspring. This is called *natural selection*. With successive generations the advantageous genes will spread through the population.

Organisms live in environments that change constantly, and individuals with characteristics that best suit the prevailing conditions will survive at the expense of those that are not suited. Over successive generations these favourable characteristics (adaptations) will accumulate (by natural selection) and eventually cause the organism to alter. This is *evolution*.

When Madagascar became isolated from Africa, conditions on the new island were different from those on the mainland. With time, the 'founding stock' of animals and plants evolved in response to their new circumstances, to become new species (a process called *speciation*). And because Madagascar was isolated there were no diluting influences from the mainland, so the new species could develop in unique ways. However, some species on Madagascar do show some similarities to species in other parts of the world. For example, the mantella frogs look and behave very much like the poison-arrow frogs from Central and South America, even though they are only distantly related. Both live similar lifestyles under similar conditions, so natural selection has independently arrived at a solution: this is called *convergent evolution*.

This may also happen to unrelated organisms living in the same area, where they develop common characteristics (through convergent evolution) and then continue to evolve along similar lines, so that their resemblances become quite striking: this is called *parallel evolution*. For example, the true sunbirds and sunbird-asties on Madagascar.

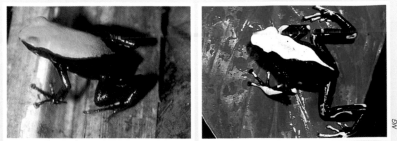

Above left The green-backed mantella frog, Madagascar.

Above right Poison-arrow frog, South America. Unrelated, yet so similar: an example of convergent evolution.

WHAT'S IN A NAME?

TECHNICAL TERMS

We have made every effort to keep the text in this book accessible. However, the use of some technical terms has been essential to fully explain certain aspects of natural history. The following definitions will unravel any mysteries.

Nocturnal Animals active only under cover of darkness (at night).

Diurnal Animals active only during the daylight hours.

Cathemeral Animals that are active both by day and by night.

Crepuscular Animals that confine their activity to the twilight hours around dusk and dawn.

Larva The immature stage in an insect's lifecycle between the egg and the pupa, eg caterpillar or maggot. The pupa then undergoes complete metamorphosis into a mature adult.

Nymph The immature stages of insects that resemble the adult forms and develop in gradual steps, eg crickets and grasshoppers.

Hibernate Where animals lower their metabolic rate and become torpid in response to cold (normally winter). They survive on fat reserves laid down during the summer.

Aestivate Where animals enter torpor in response to a dry season, also living on fat reserves.

Endemic A species (or other taxonomic group) that is restricted to a particular geographic region, often due to isolation, as with islands. Both taxon and region must be defined, eg crowned lemurs are endemic to northern Madagascar, while their family, Lemuridae, is endemic to the island as a whole.

Indigenous A species (or other taxonomic group) that naturally occurs in a particular region, but that also naturally occurs in other regions, eg pied crows are found throughout sub-Saharan Africa but also Madagascar and are indigenous to both areas.

Exotic A species (or other taxonomic group) that has been either deliberately or accidentally introduced to a region to which it is not indigenous.

Niche The role of an organism within its physical environment and with respect to the communities of other organisms that share its environment.

Gene The segments of DNA contained in cells that carry the blueprints (in code form) for building all living organisms.

CLASSIFICATION

Biologists have created a strict set of rules to identify organisms precisely. This is called classification or taxonomy and an understanding of its principles will help clarify the descriptions in this book.

The first division, called a kingdom, is very broadly defined, for instance animal, plant or fungi. Each subsequent division then becomes more precisely defined, until the organism is identified: this is called the species. Here are two simplified examples from Madagascar.

Ring-tailed lemur		**Parson's chameleon**	
Kingdom:	Animalia	Kingdom:	Animalia
Phylum:	Chordata	Phylum:	Chordata
Class:	Mammalia	Class:	Reptilia
Order:	Primates	Order:	Squamata
Family:	Lemuridae	Family:	Chamaeleonidae
Subfamily:	Lemurinae	Subfamily:	Chamaeleoninae
Genus:	*Lemur*	Genus:	*Calumma*
Species:	*catta*	Species:	*parsonii*

The different chapters in this book broadly relate to different Classes of animals, for instance mammals (Mammalia), birds (Aves) and reptiles (Reptilia). Given in Latin or Greek, the universal languages of biologists, only the genus (plural: genera) and species are quoted. This constitutes the 'scientific name' and is written in italics. The genus name always begins in upper case, while the species name is written entirely in lower case. If the genus is known, but not the species, it will be written thus: *Lemur* sp., or if the description includes several members of the same genus (congeners), it will be written: *Lemur* spp.

The scientific name often gives useful information about the animal's appearance, preferred habitat, where it lives or who discovered it. Take, for example, the red-bellied lemur (*Eulemur rubriventer*): *rubri* means red, while *venter* means belly. If the species name is *occidentalis*, then the animal is from western Madagascar, while you can deduce that the golden-crowned sifaka (*Propithecus tattersalli*) was named after the primatologist Ian Tattersall.

Furthermore some species are divided into subspecies or races. Often these groups have been separated for long periods, perhaps by geographical barriers, and evolution has changed, say, their colour (although they could interbreed to produce hybrids were their populations to come together again). The subspecies name is written after the species name. For example in the brown lemur, the benchmark or 'nominate' race is *Eulemur fulvus fulvus*, plus five other subspecies, the red-fronted brown lemur (*Eulemur fulvus rufus*), Sanford's brown lemur (*Eulemur fulvus sanfordi*), white-fronted brown lemur (*Eulemur fulvus albifrons*), white-collared brown lemur (*Eulemur fulvus albocollaris*) and collared brown lemur (*Eulemur fulvus collaris*).

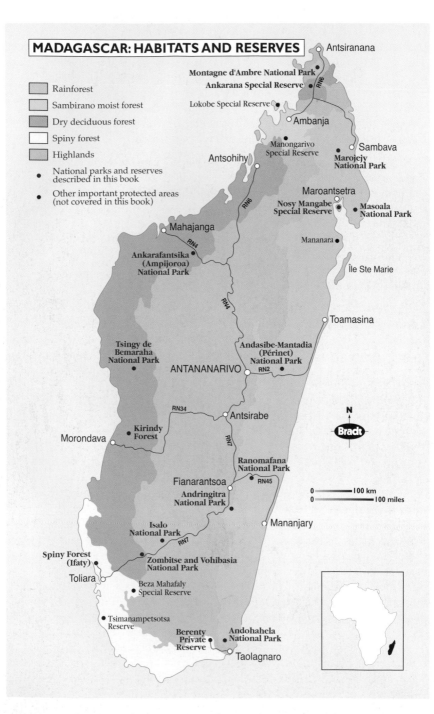

MADAGASCAR: HABITATS AND RESERVES

Antsiranana

Rainforest

Sambirano moist forest

Dry deciduous forest

Spiny forest

Highlands

● National parks and reserves described in this book

● Other important protected areas (not covered in this book)

Montagne d'Ambre National Park
Ankarana Special Reserve
Lokobe Special Reserve

RN6

Ambanja

Antsohihy

Manongarivo Special Reserve

Sambava

Marojejy National Park

Maroantsetra

Nosy Mangabe Special Reserve

Masoala National Park

Mananara

Mahajanga

RN4

Ankarafantsika (Ampijoroa) National Park

Île Ste Marie

RN4

Toamasina

Tsingy de Bemaraha National Park

Andasibe-Mantadia (Périnet) National Park

ANTANANARIVO

RN2

N

Bradt

RN34

Antsirabe

Kirindy Forest

Morondava

RN7

Ranomafana National Park

Fianarantsoa

RN45

Andringitra National Park

0 —— 100 km
0 —— 100 miles

Isalo National Park

Mananjary

RN7

Spiny Forest (Ifaty)

Zombitse and Vohibasia National Park

Toliara

Beza Mahafaly Special Reserve

Tsimanampetsotsa Reserve

Berenty Private Reserve

Andohahela National Park

Taolagnaro

HABITATS
AND RESERVES

Lac Vert, Andasibe

Ranomafana National Park

RAINFOREST

The eastern rainforest is a treasure chest for naturalists as it supports the greatest number of animal and plant species in Madagascar. To visitors more familiar with temperate woodlands, where one or two species like beech or maple dominate, the diversity of plants in a small area of tropical rainforest is bewildering. In Madagascar botanists are still classifying the flora: palm specialists have recently discovered many new species, and orchids, for which the island is famous, are also receiving considerable attention.

Evergreen rainforest in Madagascar has different characteristics depending on altitude and rainfall. Most of the protected areas described here fall into the two categories outlined below.

Lowland rainforest lies below 800m and is drenched with an average 3,500mm of rain per year. It is similar to rainforest growing in other tropical regions, with large trees supported by buttress roots, smaller trees with stilt-like aerial roots, saplings, lianas, epiphytes and ferns. Compared with other continents, however, the trees are closer together and the canopy lower, and there are fewer tall trees poking their crowns above the rest. Species of *Impatiens* are common here.

Montane rainforest is typical of key reserves like Andasibe-Mantadia (Périnet), Ranomafana and Montagne d'Ambre (Amber Mountain). It is found between 800m and about 1,300m, above which it is called high altitude montane forest. Tree ferns are a feature of montane forests and bamboo is common, as are species of *Kalanchoe*. Compared with lowland rainforest, leaves are smaller and tougher, mosses and epiphytes are more abundant, and shrubby undergrowth flourishes as more light reaches the forest floor.

The majority of Madagascar's rainforests are concentrated in a band, known as the Madagascar Sylva, which extends from around Iharana (Vohemar) in the north all the way down to Taolagnaro (Fort Dauphin) in the south. Once continuous, this band of forest has been severely fragmented by the timber industry, and – more importantly – through the slash-and-burn agricultural practices of the land-hungry rural people.

Other isolated patches of montane forest occur towards the island's northern tip around Montagne d'Ambre. A further area of moist forest in the northwest, the Sambirano Domain, constitutes a transition between eastern rainforests and western deciduous forests. The main block is centred around Manangorivo and part of the Tsarantanana Massif, but it also extends to the coast and includes the forests on Nosy Be and some of its surrounding islands.

MONTAGNE D'AMBRE (AMBER MOUNTAIN) NATIONAL PARK

Montagne d'Ambre is a green oasis: Antsiranana (Diego Suarez) receives only about 900mm of rain per year, but the park is drenched with an average of 3,585mm. This is a particularly rewarding reserve for the average visitor. It is easy to get to, has a good trail system, labelled trees and points of interest (some in English), and is very beautiful. Lemurs are usually seen and reptiles are abundant, with a wonderful array of chameleons.

Habitat and Terrain

Montagne d'Ambre is an isolated patch of montane rainforest covering an area of 18,200ha and lying at altitudes between 850m and 1,475m. It derives its name from the resin that oozes from some of its trees, a few of which reach 40m. The park is notable for its bird's nest ferns, tree ferns, orchids, mosses and lianas. Two waterfalls form the focal points, and there are crater lakes and viewpoints over the forest and surrounding area.

Key Species

Mammals Sanford's brown lemur, crowned lemur, northern sportive lemur, Amber Mountain fork-marked lemur, brown mouse lemur, northern ring-tailed mongoose and fosa. The rare falanouc has been seen here.

Birds Madagascar crested ibis, Madagascar malachite kingfisher, Madagascar blue pigeon, Amber Mountain rock-thrush, Madagascar magpie-robin, cuckoo-roller, pitta-like ground roller, Madagascar paradise flycatcher, souimanga sunbird, Madagascar white-throated rail, white-throated oxylabes, spectacled greenbul, hook-billed vanga, dark newtonia.

Reptiles and frogs Look for Madagascar tree boa, Boettger's chameleon, panther chameleon, stump-tailed chameleons, *Brookesia tuberculata*, *B. decaryi*, and *B. stumpffi*, three leaf-tailed geckos, *Uroplatus sikorae* and *U. ebenaui*, and two day geckos, *Phelsuma madagascariensis grandis* and *P. lineata dorsivittata*.

Visitor Information

Location 27km south of Antsiranana (Diego Suarez).

Access The road is tarred as far as Ambohitra (Joffreville); the last 7km is well-maintained dirt road. In wet months tracks in the park are unsuitable for most vehicles. Footpaths are clearly marked.

Best months to visit Accessible and rewarding at any time of year. More comfortable in the drier months (May to November) but better for wildlife between September and April, although rain can be heavy.

Accommodation Two very good lodges in nearby Joffrevile; dormitory (must be pre-booked) and campsite in the park.

Grading Easy. Much can be seen in the vicinity of the campsite/car park. Longer trails may be steep and rugged and leeches are a problem after rain.

Recommendations Stay at least one night. On a brief visit make the short walk to the Petite Cascade (small waterfall) and along the botanical trail for a cross-section of wildlife.

NG

OB

Above Grande Cascade, Montagne d'Ambre National Park. The walk to this waterfall gives a good cross-section of the park's attractions, both plant and animal.

Left The brilliantly coloured Madagascar malachite kingfisher (*Corythornis vintsioides*) is often seen by the stream leading from the Petite Cascade.

11

MAROJEJY NATIONAL PARK

Marojejy lies towards the northern extreme of the rainforest belt and comprises some of the most remote and hitherto unexplored areas within this region. The relative inaccessibility is in part due to the ruggedness of this mountainous massif. The area's fauna and flora is extremely rich and diverse. Virtually all rainforest bird species from Madagascar have been recorded in and around Marojejy and the adjoining forests, no less than ten lemur species are known from the area and there are countless reptiles and frogs, many of which are almost certainly new to science. Until recently the area was closed to all but official research personnel; however, the park came into being in November 1998 facilitating the first tourist access and it was officially inaugurated in June 2000.

Habitat and Terrain

The variation in altitude results in considerable habitat diversity, from dense lowland rainforests at lower elevations, where the canopy exceeds 30m, to moist montane scrub and even ericoid moorland close to the peaks. The terrain is demanding and gradients are often very steep. Annual rainfall exceeds 4,000mm and there is no obvious dry season.

Key Species

Mammals Silky sifaka, white-fronted brown lemur, red-bellied lemur, eastern grey bamboo lemur, greater dwarf lemur, eastern woolly lemur, weasel sportive lemur, brown mouse lemur and aye-aye. Other mammals include fanaloka, fosa, ring-tailed mongoose, red forest rat and lowland streaked tenrec.

Birds Helmet vanga, Bernier's vanga, red-tailed vanga, velvet asity, common sunbird asity, yellow-bellied sunbird asity, short-legged ground roller, scaly ground roller, rufous-headed ground roller, blue coua, red-fronted coua, red-breasted coua and cuckoo roller.

Reptiles and frogs Three species of leaf-tailed gecko: *Uroplatus fimbriatus, U. phantasicus,* and *U. Lineatus* Short-horned chameleon, Boettger's chameleon, stump-tailed chameleons (*Brookesia* sp.), Madagascar tree boa, and a myriad of frogs belonging to the genera *Boophis, Mantidactylus,* and *Mantella.*

Visitor Information

Location Marojejy lies directly to the north of Andapa, 70km inland from the coastal town of Sambava in northeast Madagascar.

Access Via the village of Manantenina on the Sambava to Andapa road. From Manantenina the park boundary is around two hours on foot. Trails have recently been improved, but they are still narrow, often steep and can be slippery after rain.

Best Months to Visit October to December. November and early December are likely to have the least rain. Avoid the cyclone season from January to early April.

Accommodation The first camp (450m) is a 2-hour walk from the park boundary, and the second (750m) is a further hour. Both have huts with bunks and flushing toilets. Camp 3 (1,380m) requires tents.

Grading Very difficult. Humid, often wet, steep trails.

Recommendations A minimum stay of 3 days. Areas around Camp One are best for helmet vanga; forests above Camp Two are more likely for silky sifaka. Guides and excursions can be arranged through WWF in Andapa.

NG

Above The Marojejy massif, a rugged mountain area where peaks rise to 2,137m, and are amongst the highest on the island.

Left Helmet vanga (*Euryceros prevostii*) arriving at its nest. Marojejy is one of the few places where this spectacular bird may be seen.

NG

13

MASOALA NATIONAL PARK

The Masoala peninsula has the largest remaining area of coastal/lowland rainforest on Madagascar, often extending right down to the shore. The peninsula covers a total area in excess of 400,000ha with the park occupying 210,200ha of largely primary forest.

Masoala has arguably the greatest biodiversity in all of Madagascar and efforts to conserve it against the encroachment of agriculture and logging are of vital importance. Fortunately several conservation bodies are active in the region. The national park includes a small marine reserve.

Habitat and Terrain

The height of the canopy is around 30m and there are few emergent trees. The understorey is characterised by abundant palms and tree ferns and there are many epiphytes and orchids. The slopes are often very steep, and there are numerous clear, fast flowing streams and small rivers. This is the wettest part of Madagascar: annual rainfall exceeds 5,000mm and there is no distinct dry season.

Key Species

Mammals The only place to see red-ruffed lemur; also present are white-fronted brown lemur, eastern woolly lemur, aye-aye, brown mouse lemur, fosa, fanaloka, falanouc, brown-tailed mongoose, greater hedgehog tenrec and lowland streaked tenrec.

Birds Much sought after, but very difficult to see are Madagascar serpent eagle, Madagascar red owl and Bernier's vanga. Regularly seen are helmet and nuthatch vangas, red-breasted coua, scaly ground roller, short-legged ground roller, Madagascar wood rail and velvet asity.

Reptiles and frogs Various chameleons including panther chameleon, hooded chameleon (*Calumma cucullata*), several species of stump-tailed chameleon, at least two leaf-tailed geckos, *Uroplatus fimbriatus* and *U. lineatus*, numerous day geckos (*Phelsuma* sp.), tomato frog (*Dyscophus antongili*) and the green-backed mantella (*Mantella laevigata*).

Visitor Information

Location The peninsula lies to the east of Maroantsetra and forms the northern coastline of the Bay of Antongil in northeast Madagascar.

Access Only accessible by boat, around 2-3 hours from Maroantsetra. The best areas of forest, with a good trail system, are near Andranobe or Tampolo.

Best months to visit September to December. November is the most likely month for a few dry days. Masoala is wet throughout the year, but dry spells are possible anytime. Avoid the cyclone season (January to March) as the boat journey is dangerous in heavy seas.

Accommodation Basic lodges at Tampolo; campsites only at Ambanizana and Lohatrozona. All equipment and provisions must be brought from Maroantsetra.

Grading Difficult. Hot, humid, often very wet with steep trails.

Recommendations A visit of at least 3 days is recommended for this wonderful area. Hotels in Maroantsetra can arrange boats, equipment and excursions. A local guide from the Association des Guides Ecotouristiques de Maroantsetra (AGEM) is essential at all times.

Above Red ruffed lemur (*Varecia variegata rubra*) in Masoala National Park. This is a beautiful example of lowland rainforest, which is home to numerous endemic species.

Left Scaly ground roller (*Brachypteracias squamigera*), one of Masoala's many rare endemic birds.

NOSY MANGABE SPECIAL RESERVE

An island in the Bay of Antongil, Nosy Mangabe has been a popular centre for research since 1966 when several aye-ayes were released. Groups of black-and-white ruffed lemurs and brown lemurs were also introduced prior to this and these species have subsequently thrived. Some of the species from Masoala and elsewhere on the mainland can be seen more readily here and access is more straightforward.

Habitat and Terrain

Lowland rainforest covers the entire island, some 520ha. This forest has largely regenerated after considerable logging around 200 years ago. There are large buttress-rooted trees reaching 35m or more in height. Species typical of this type of forest include: *Ravensara*, *Canarium*, *Ocotea*, *Ficus* and *Tambourissa*. Tree ferns, ferns, epiphytes and orchids are also common. The island's slopes rise steeply from the sea to the summit at 331m.

Key Species

Mammals This is a possible place to see an aye-aye. Other lemurs: black and white ruffed lemur, white-fronted brown lemur and brown mouse lemur. Also greater hedgehog tenrec and Commerson's leaf-nosed bat.

Birds Not particularly diverse or abundant. Madagascar paradise flycatcher, Madagascar bulbul and Madagascar malachite kingfisher are common. On the coastal rocks look for Madagascar pratincoles and dark phase dimorphic egrets around the shoreline.

Reptiles and frogs The best place to see the leaf-tailed gecko (*Uroplatus fimbriatus*), which is common. Also, pygmy stump-tailed chameleon (*Brookesia peyrierasi*), panther chameleon, several day geckos (*Phelsuma* sp.) and plated lizards (*Zonosaurus madagascariensis* and *Z. brygooi*). Frogs include green-backed mantella (*Mantella laevigata*) and several other ground- and tree-dwelling species.

Visitor Information

Location The island lies 5km off Maroantsetra in the Bay of Antongil.

Access The boat from Maroantsetra takes 40 minutes. An extensive trail system runs from the campsite and covers most of the island.

Best months to visit Accessible all year around, but avoid the cyclone season (January to March) as the sea can be very choppy. The best time to try and see aye-ayes on trees near the beach is between April and June.

Accommodation A well-maintained campsite behind the beach, with covered platforms for tents, a cold shower (fed from a waterfall) and flushing toilets. All equipment and provisions must be brought from Maroantsetra.

Grading Moderate. The path behind the beach is flat. All others trails are steep and can be very slippery after rain.

Recommendations A day trip from Maroantsetra, leaving early in the morning, is possible and will be rewarding. However, it is recommended that at least one night be spent camping, particularly if hoping to see the nocturnal aye-aye.

Above A sandy beach at Nosy Mangabe.

Left Aye-aye (*Daubentonia madagascariensis*). In 1966, when the aye-aye was thought to be on the brink of extinction, nine of these lemurs were released on Nosy Mangabe – the ancestors of today's population.

ANDASIBE-MANTADIA NATIONAL PARK (PÉRINET)

This park is an amalgamation of Analamazaotra Special Reserve close to the town of Andasibe (Périnet) and the more recently created Mantadia National Park that lies nearby. In combination, this is now perhaps Madagascar's premier rainforest reserve, offering the chance of close encounters with various lemurs and an opportunity to glimpse some of the island's highly sought after rarities. The old Special Reserve remains the place to see and hear the indri, while in Mantadia can be seen diademed sifaka, black-and-white ruffed lemur and four species of ground roller.

Although unprotected, the nearby rainforest of Maromizaha is rewarding, especially for invertebrates. There are also superb views from the lookout point.

Habitat and Terrain

The reserve at Andasibe is a fragment of mid-altitude montane rainforest covering an area of 810ha at altitudes between 930 and 1,040m. Many of the largest trees have been removed and the canopy averages 25–30m. The main area is centred on a ridge with some steep slopes descending to a small dammed lake, Lac Vert.

Mantadia is a superb example of lowland and mid-altitude rainforest lying between 800m and 1,260m and extending to 10,000ha. Towering buttress-rooted trees rising to 35m dominate lower elevations, and tree ferns (*Cyathea* sp.) form a significant part of the understorey. At higher elevations the forest is more stunted and moss and lichen growth is luxuriant. There is little or no flat ground and many of the slopes are very steep.

Key species

Mammals Indri, diademed sifaka (Mantadia), common brown lemur, red bellied lemur, black and white ruffed lemur (Mantadia), grey bamboo lemur. At night: brown mouse lemur, greater dwarf lemur, eastern woolly lemur and hairy-eared dwarf lemur. Also lowland streaked tenrec, red forest rat and eastern ring-tailed mongoose.

Birds Blue coua, red-fronted coua, blue vanga, red-tailed vanga, nuthatch vanga, tylas vanga, white-headed vanga, velvet asity, sunbird asity, pitta-like ground roller, rufous-headed ground roller, scaly ground roller (Mantadia), short-legged ground roller (Mantadia), cuckoo roller, collared nightjar, Madagascar long-eared owl and cryptic warbler.

Reptiles and frogs Parson's chameleon (*Calumma parsonii*), short-horned chameleon (*Calumma brevicornis*), short-nosed chameleon (*Calumma gastrotaenia*) and nose-horned chameleon (*Calumma nasuta*). Also stump-tailed chameleon (*Brookesia supercilliaris*), 'mossy' leaf-tailed gecko (*Uroplatus sikorae*) and Madagascar tree boa. Frogs include golden mantella (*Mantella aurantica*) (in areas close to the reserve), painted mantella (*Mantella madagascariensis*) (Mantadia) and many others belonging to the genera *Boophis* and *Mantidactylus*.

Visitor Information

Location 30km east of Moramanga and approximately 145km east of Antananarivo off the main road (RN2) between Antananarivo and Toamasina (Tamatave). Mantadia lies around 20km to the north of Andasibe.

Access From Antananarivo, 4 hours by car. An extensive network of well-maintained trails criss-cross the main reserve. Mantadia is 40 minutes' drive along a dirt road from

Andasibe. Several new trails have been cut making access easier; however, many are still steep and very slippery when wet. It is always best to engage a local guide; here they are amongst the most knowledgeable and well organised in Madagascar.

Best months to visit September to end of December, April and May. Avoid the cyclone months of February and March. The wildlife is less active during the winter period of June to August.

Accommodation Several comfortable hotels; camping.

Grading Andasibe: easy/moderate. Mantadia: moderate/difficult. Accommodation is moderate to very good, while trails vary between flat and very steep.

Recommendations One day including the evening is sufficient to see the indri and the main reserve. A second (and third) day is necessary to fully explore Mantadia. A guide is obligatory.

NG

OB

Above Lac Vert at Andasibe (Périnet).

Left Indri (*Indri indri*) the 'piebald teddy-bear' whose song enthrals visitors. Indri live in small family groups; their morning calls are answered by groups up to 3km away.

RANOMAFANA NATIONAL PARK

This very beautiful national park was established in 1991 to protect the newly discovered golden bamboo lemur. It has subsequently turned out to be one of the most important wildlife sites in Madagascar and its pleasant climate, waterfalls and rushing river, and the variety of species, make it a deserved favourite.

This is perhaps the best reserve for lemur diversity; no fewer than 12 species are present, many of which can be easily be seen around the main trail systems. Reptiles and frogs are also abundant and new species are still being discovered on a regular basis. More than 100 species of birds have been identified, with 36 endemic.

Habitat and Terrain

Ranomafana's protected montane rainforest covers an area of 41,600ha, at altitudes between 800m and 1,200m. The area is dominated by the Namorona river which, fed by many streams flowing from the hills, plunges from the eastern escarpment close to the park entrance. The steep slopes are covered with a mixture of primary and secondary forest; much of the secondary growth is dominated by dense stands of introduced Strawberry guava and clumps of giant bamboo.

Key Species

Mammals Most notable are golden bamboo lemur, greater bamboo lemur, Eastern grey bamboo lemur, Milne-Edwards' sifaka, red-bellied lemur, red-fronted brown lemur, and brown mouse lemur. Others include the fanaloka, eastern ring-tailed mongoose, and red forest rat.

Birds Blue coua, red-fronted coua, Pollen's vanga, tylas vanga, velvet asity, common sunbird asity, yellow-bellied sunbird asity, pitta-like ground roller, scaly ground roller, short-legged ground roller, rufous-headed ground roller, brown mesite, Henst's goshawk, Madagascar flufftail, slender-billed flufftail, forest rock-thrush, collared nightjar, common jery, green jery and cryptic warbler.

Reptiles and frogs Parson's chameleon, and the similar-looking O'Shaughnessy's chameleon, short-horned chameleon (*Calumma brevicornis*), Madagascar tree boa, three leaf-tailed geckos, *Uroplatus fimbriatus*, *U. sikorae* and *U. phantasticus*, the day gecko *Phelsuma quadriocellata* (common) and numerous frogs belonging to the genera *Boophis* and *Mantidactylus*. The painted mantella (*Mantella madagascariensis*) is found here.

Visitor Information

Location Approximately 65km northeast of Fianarantsoa.

Access Via the poor road that connects Fianarantsoa with Mananjary on the east coast, a 2-hour journey from Fianarantsoa. There is an extensive system of trails and paths, but many follow steep and often muddy slopes.

Best months to visit The summer rainy season (December to March) is the most rewarding, but access and conditions can be difficult. Otherwise the periods either side of the main rains: April and September to November.

Accommodation Two comfortable hotels and three rustic guesthouses in Ranomafana, along with dormitory accommodation at the entrance to the park. Campsites close to the park entrance.

Grading Moderate/difficult. Accommodation is not luxurious and many of the trails are steep and slippery after rain. Leaches are common.

Recommendations The minimum stay is one night, allowing an afternoon or night walk and a morning excursion. For enthusiasts, two or three days, with an all-day excursion and at least one night-time visit.

Above Namorona Falls, Ranomafana National Park.

Left Milne-Edwards' sifaka (*Propithecus diadema edwardsi*), a subspecies of the diademed sifaka (also known by their Malagasy name, simpona). Simpona vary greatly in colouring, and are the largest of the sifakas, some subspecies being only slightly smaller than the indri.

Giant baobabs *(Adansonia grandidieri)* near Morondava

DRY DECIDUOUS FOREST

The deciduous forests of western Madagascar are less rich in species than the rainforests of the east, but nonetheless contain a wealth of fauna and flora that is of great importance, including some of Madagascar's most endangered animals. The rate of endemicity is higher here than in the east, though the number of species is smaller. The large trees have adapted to a prolonged dry season by shedding their leaves to prevent moisture loss through evaporation. Some, like the baobabs which are such a feature of this area, store water in their bulbous trunks, hence the name 'bottle trees'. Others have roots that are swollen with water to tide them through the drought.

Forests are described as having 'storeys' or layers of vegetation showing different characteristics. Dry western forests have an understorey comprised of very dense shrubs and saplings, many of which keep their leaves during the rainless months, and an upper storey of large trees up to 20m tall which lose their leaves in the dry season. The middle storey has features from both.

Deciduous forest is found on the coastal plain and associated limestone plateaux from sea level to 800m, stretching from Antsiranana (Diego Suarez) at the island's northern tip to Morombe in the southwest. Like the eastern rainforest they have been ravaged by man and are now only found in discontinuous patches, being replaced by largely sterile coarse savannah grassland. This destruction is of particular concern since the trees grow extremely slowly in this zone. The dry season extends from May to October, but there are considerable differences in rainfall between areas: only about 500mm falls annually in the southwest, whereas the extreme north receives up to 2,000mm.

Within the region there are a number of limestone plateaux that have been eroded into spectacular pinnacle formations known as karst or locally as 'tsingy' (the sound the rock makes when struck). Through these plateaux flow rivers which have created underground passages and caves, some of which have collapsed to form canyons in which forest often flourishes. The main examples of this are at Ankarana and Bemaraha.

Choosing the best time to visit the western forests is difficult. By far the most pleasant months physically are May to September when it is dry and relatively cool, but wildlife is difficult to see. As the rainy season progresses so the humidity rises and insects, particularly flies, become increasingly persistent. When the discomfort is at its worst, December to March, the wildlife – especially reptiles – is at its best. Late September to December is – overall – the most rewarding period.

ANKARANA SPECIAL RESERVE

This is one of the most adventurous reserves for visitors, rewarding those who make the effort with a dramatic landscape of limestone pinnacles (tsingy), caves, untouched forest and a wealth of wildlife.

Habitat and Terrain

The Ankarana Massif is a limestone plateau approximately 5km x 20km, which rises abruptly from the surrounding grassy plain. Some of the largest caves have collapsed, permitting isolated pockets of river-fed forest. Dry deciduous forest grows around the periphery of the massif and penetrates up into the larger canyons.

Key Species

Mammals Crowned lemur, Sanford's brown lemur, northern sportive lemur and grey mouse lemur. Also northern ring-tailed mongoose, fanaloka, fosa and many bat species.

Birds White-breasted mesite, crested coua, hook-billed vanga, Madagascar crested ibis, Madagascar pygmy kingfisher, Madagascar harrier hawk and Madagascar scops owl.

Reptiles Oustalet's chameleon, white-lipped chameleon (*Furcifer minor*), big-headed gecko, (*Paroedura bastardi*), two leaf-tailed geckos, *Uroplatus henkeli* and *U. ebenaui*, the day gecko *Phelsuma madagascariensis grandis* and Madagascar ground boa.

Visitor Information

Location Approximately 110km south of Antsiranana (Diego Suarez).

Access The four campsites can be reached by 4WD vehicles, but most visitors prefer the three-hour hike from RN6. A guide is obligatory.

Best months to visit Wildlife is more visible in the hot, wet months.

Accommodation Camping only, but rooms are available on the perimeter of the reserve.

Grading Difficult. Tough hiking, basic camping; high temperatures.

Recommendations Stay at least two, preferably three nights. Plan to climb to the Green Lake (Lac Vert) and its surrounding area of 'tsingy'. Tiring, but well worth it.

TSINGY DE BEMARAHA NATIONAL PARK

This remote and little-known limestone region became a national park in 1998.

Habitat and Terrain

This is the second largest protected area on the island. The razor-sharp 'tsingy' forms an impenetrable fortress in places, while the Manambolo River cuts a spectacular gorge through the limestone.

Key species

Mammals Decken's sifaka, red-fronted brown lemur, grey mouse lemur, fat-tailed dwarf lemur and Milne-Edward's sportive lemur.

Birds Coquerel's coua, sickle-billed vanga, white-headed vanga and rufous vanga.

Reptiles Madagascar ground boa, stump-tailed chameleon (*Brookesia perarmata*), leaf-tailed gecko (*Uroplatus guentheri*) and big-headed gecko (*Paroedura picta*).

Visitor Information

Location Some 100km northeast of Belo Tsirihibina, north of the Manambolo River.

Access Via Bekopaka by 4x4: 10 hours from Morondava; by air to Antsalova in the north.

Best months to visit August to December.

Accommodation Basic hotels in Bekopaka and Antsalova; camping.

Grading Moderate to difficult. Can be very hot.

Recommendations Excursions and flights by light aircraft can be arranged through hotels in Morondava. Rafting trips down the Manambolo River finish at Bemaraha.

Above 'Tsingy' at Ankarana.

Left Female crowned lemur (*Eulemur coronatus*) and baby. Crowned lemurs are semi-tame at Ankarana and hang around the campsite looking for handouts (they should not be fed). Ring-tailed mongooses are equally bold.

25

AMPIJOROA FORESTRY STATION (ANKARAFANTSIKA NATIONAL PARK)

Ampijoroa competes with Kirindy in providing the best accessible example of western deciduous forest. Access is easy and a clear network of level paths makes wildlife viewing easy. Many groups of lemurs have become tolerant of people so can be observed at close quarters. Night walks are particularly rewarding as the density of nocturnal lemurs is high. Birdwatching is also outstanding with a number of rare endemics, such as Schlegel's asity, Madagascar fish eagle and Van Dam's vanga frequently seen.

Habitat and Terrain

The newly created Ankarafantsika National Park is still generally known by its old name, Ampijoroa. Lac Ravelobe lies on the northern side of the road. Around the lake, on sandy soil, grows typical dry deciduous forest. The understorey is sparse, with few epiphytes but abundant lianas. In the rocky, more open areas succulents like elephant's foot plants (*Pachypodium* spp.) and *Aloe* species grow. The terrain is gently undulating or flat, with the occasional shallow ridge. Trails are broad and hiking is easy.

Key Species

Mammals Coquerel's sifaka, mongoose lemur, common brown lemur, western woolly lemur, Milne-Edwards' sportive lemur, fat-tailed dwarf lemur, grey mouse lemur and golden-brown mouse lemur.

Birds Best place to see the rare Madagascar fish eagle and white-breasted mesite. Also red-capped coua, Coquerel's coua, crested coua, Madagascar green pigeon, Schlegel's asity, Van Dam's vanga, rufous vanga, sickle-billed vanga, greater vasa parrot and Madagascar pygmy kingfisher.

Reptiles Oustalet's chameleon, rhinoceros chameleon, stump-tailed chameleon (*Brookesia decaryi*), iguanid lizards (*Oplurus* sp.), two leaf-tailed geckos, *Uroplatus henkeli* and *U. guentheri*, fish-scaled gecko, Madagascar ground boa, giant hog-nosed snake, spear-nosed snake and 'fandrefiala' (*Ithycyphus miniatus*). The lake is home to Nile crocodiles. There is a captive-breeding programme for the plowshare tortoise (angonoka), flat-tailed tortoise (kapidolo) and Madagascar big-headed (side-necked) turtle.

Visitor Information

Location The Ampijoroa Forestry Station lies either side of RN4 approximately 120km southeast of Mahajanga (Majunga).

Access The road from Mahajanga is good and the journey takes around 2 hours. Excellent guides are usually available in the reserve.

Best months to visit The reptiles are more prominent after the first rains in November. During the summer (December to March), however, it can be extremely hot.

Accommodation Comfortable rooms must be booked through an agent. Basic accommodation and a campsite are also available.

Grading Moderate. Easy if taken as a day trip in the cool months.

Recommendations Spend at least one night for the best birdwatching and wildlife viewing, or aim to leave Mahajanga before dawn.

NG

AA

Above Lac Ravelobe, Ampijoroa. There is a good chance of seeing the highly endangered Madagascar fish eagle around this lake.

Left Coquerel's sifaka, (*Propithecus verreauxi coquereli*), and infant. Born in June and July, the baby is at first carried on its mother's front, clinging to her fur. When it is about a month old it rides on her back. These beautiful lemurs are easily seen in Ampijoroa.

KIRINDY FOREST

This is one of the most rewarding wildlife habitats on Madagascar, and yet it is not part of the network of national parks and reserves. The area was formerly administered by the Coopération Suisse, having been established as an experiment in sustainable commercial logging. Controlled timber extraction appears to have had little effect on the abundance and diversity of wildlife and Kirindy remains the best place to look for a number of endemic dry forest species like giant jumping rat, narrow-striped mongoose and pygmy mouse lemur. It is also the most likely location to see a fosa.

Habitat and Terrain

Deciduous forest covering around 10,000ha and growing on the sandy soils of the western coastal plain at altitudes between 15m and 40m. The tree species are similar to other deciduous forests of the west: the canopy normally averages 12m to 15m, but may reach 20m to 25m in the more humid areas along water courses. There is often a dense understorey and intermediate layer before the canopy. In addition there are three species of baobab, *Adansonia rubrostipa*, *A. za* and *A. grandidieri*.

Key Species

Mammals Notable for six species of nocturnal lemur: pygmy mouse lemur, grey mouse lemur, red-tailed sportive lemur, pale fork-marked lemur, Coquerel's dwarf lemur and fat-tailed dwarf lemur. Also Verreaux's sifaka and red-fronted brown lemur. Other mammals include fosa, narrow-striped mongoose, giant jumping rat, common tenrec, greater hedgehog tenrec and large-eared tenrec.

Birds White-breasted mesite, Coquerel's coua, crested coua, sickle-bill vanga, white-headed vanga, rufous vanga, blue vanga, Chabert's vanga, cuckoo roller, Madagascar harrier hawk, Henst's goshawk and banded kestrel.

Reptiles Flat-tailed tortoise (kapidolo), Madagascar ground boa, giant hog-nosed snake, spear-nosed snake (*Langaha madagascariensis*), plated lizards (*Zonosaurus* sp.), Oustalet's chameleon, Labord's chameleon (*Furcifer labordi*), leaf-tailed gecko (*Uroplatus guentheri*), big-headed gecko (*Paroedura picta*) and several day geckos including *Phelsuma madagascariensis kochi* and *P. mutabilis*.

Visitor Information

Location Approximately 65km northeast of Morondava and on the eastern side of the road to Belo Sur Tsiribihina.

Access The drive from Morondava, via the 'Avenue of Baobabs', takes about 2 hours on a reasonable dirt road. Trails within the forest are generally wide and mainly flat.

Best months to visit October to December, before it gets too hot and wet. Avoid June to August when some animals aestivate or are less active.

Accommodation Campsite plus basic huts and bunk accommodation.

Grading Moderate. Basic facilities, easy walking, but can be very hot.

Recommendations One or two nights' camping is recommended to make the most of the nocturnal wildlife for which Kirindy is renowned. Local forestry staff can be hired as guides.

NG

HB

Above A broad trail in Kirindy.

Left The giant jumping rat (*Hypogeomys antimena*), known locally as 'Vositse', is only found in this small area of Madagascar. When in a hurry it jumps like a small wallaby, but when searching for its favourite food of roots and saplings it walks on all fours.

29

Didiereacaea

THE SOUTHERN REGION

This area is perhaps the most peculiar and unusual in Madagascar. It extends from Morombe in the southwest right around the southern coast and almost as far as Taolagnaro (Fort Dauphin), and inland for a distance up to 50km. The vegetation comprises a type of deciduous thicket or thorn scrub dominated by members of the family Didiereaceae and species of Euphorbia. This is commonly referred to as 'spiny forest' or 'spiny desert'.

Didiereaceae resemble cacti and are an excellent example of parallel evolution: nature comes up with similar water-retaining, predator deterring solutions to dry climates, even though their plant families are different.

Mixed in with the four genera of Didiereaceae are Euphorbias. Most ooze latex if cut or damaged, and only a few species bear thorns.

Conspicuous among these strange plants are the 'bottle trees'. These include baobabs, which tower above the thickets, and species of *Pachypodium* or 'elephant's foot' – some really do look like an elephant's foot, being squat and grey, whilst others look remarkably like a spiny bottle. All in all it's a most fascinating landscape.

Because of its arid nature, this area has suffered less than others on the island from 'slash-and-burn' agriculture. Nonetheless, the forests are becoming increasingly fragmented as the population increases with intensified pressures on the forests for charcoal, maize cultivation and building materials. While some protected areas have been set aside, there is an urgent need for a reserve to be created in the southwestern spiny forest to the north of Toliara (Tuléar); discussions are taking place on creating a new national park from Ifaty northwards. Some highly localised and threatened birds, reptiles and plants are found here.

Dry gallery forest, also called riverine forest or tamarind forest, occurs by southern rivers. This is superficially similar in appearance to western dry forest, but is dominated by huge tamarind trees (*Tamarindus indica*), locally called 'kily', which may exceed 20m. There are also sprawling banyan (*Ficus*) trees as well as an understorey of shrubs and saplings. The famous private reserve of Berenty is mainly gallery forest.

Ring-tailed lemur

BERENTY PRIVATE RESERVE

This is the best-known reserve in Madagascar. For most visitors it is infinitely rewarding, with a combination of comfortable accommodation, friendly lemurs, and easy walking in the gallery forest. In adjacent areas of spiny forest, nocturnal mouse and sportive lemurs are easily seen, sometimes even during the day. This is one of the few reserves where visitors can wander without a guide, offering a rare opportunity to be alone with the wildlife. A little to the north, the diverse spiny forest of the Anjampolo is a very good place to see sifaka and ring-tailed lemurs leaping among Didieraceae.

Habitat and Terrain

The reserve is situated on the banks of the Mandrare River and covers an area of 265ha. Adjacent to the gallery forest are areas of spiny forest. The terrain is flat.

Key Species

Mammals Ring-tailed lemur, Verreaux's sifaka, red-fronted brown lemur (introduced), grey mouse lemur, white-footed sportive lemur, lesser hedgehog tenrec, Madagascar flying fox and small Indian civet (introduced).

Birds Giant coua, hook-billed vanga, Madagascar magpie-robin, Madagascar paradise flycatcher, ashy cuckoo shrike, Frances's sparrowhawk, Madagascar sparrowhawk, grey-headed lovebird, two species of vasa parrot, Madagascar harrier hawk, Madagascar scops owl and white-browed owl.

Reptiles Radiated tortoise, spider tortoise, Dumeril's boa, warty chameleon, jewel chameleon, big-headed gecko, plated lizard (*Zonosaurus trilineatus*) and the near-limbless lizard (*Androngo trivittatus*).

Visitor Information

Location About 80km west of Taolagnaro (Fort Dauphin), just north of Amboasary.

Access With sightseeing stops, the journey from Fort Dauphin takes 3 hours on a reasonable road. There is an excellent network of wide paths and trails throughout the reserve. Guides are available, but not mandatory.

Best months to visit Accessible all year round. September and October are the months for baby lemurs; during and after the rains (December to March) for reptiles.

Accommodation A pleasant complex of bungalows with a good restaurant. This is a private reserve run by the de Heaulme family: it is necessary to book a visit through one of their hotels in Taolagnaro.

Grading Easy. This is the only reserve suitable for wheelchairs or people with disabilites.

Recommendations An expensive reserve. Feasible as a day trip, but much better to stay overnight. Best wildlife viewing is at dawn. Also take a night walk to look for invertebrates as well as nocturnal lemurs.

SG

HB

Above A troop of inquisitive ring-tailed lemurs observe the photographer on a typical Berenty trail. Ring-tails in Berenty are completely fearless and will climb all over visitors.

Left Giant coua (*Coua gigas*). Berenty provides rewarding birdwatching with several of Madagascar's endemic species easily seen.

SPINY FOREST: IFATY AND ANDOHAHELA
Although members of the Didiereaceae and Euphorbiaceae families dominate throughout, there is considerable variation within the spiny forest band. Ifaty and Andohahela lie at opposite ends of this belt, offering visitors maximum variety.

Habitat and Terrain
Growing on flat sandy coastal soils, the spiny forests near Ifaty are dominated by *Didierea madagascariensis* (see page 30) and *D. trolli*, various Euphorbia species and two species of baobab, *Adansonia rubrostipa* and *A. za*. In 'parcel 2' of Andohahela are the tall spike-like *Alluaudia procera* and *A. ascendens*. Baobab species are less common here.

IFATY
Key Species
Mammals Grey mouse lemur, white-footed sportive lemur and lesser hedgehog tenrec.

Birds Long-tailed ground roller, sub-desert mesite, Lafresnaye's vanga, sickle-bill vanga, Archbold's newtonia, thamnornis warbler, sub-desert brush warbler, olive-capped coua, running coua, Coquerel's coua, banded kestrel and Madagascar plover.

Reptiles Radiated tortoise, Dumeril's boa, iguanid lizards (*Oplurus* sp.), three-eyed lizard (*Chalaradon madagascariensis*), Oustalet's chameleon and the 'horned' chameleon.

Visitor Information
Location Inland from the village of Ifaty, about 25km north of Toliara (Tuléar).

Access The journey on a poor dirt road takes 1½ hours by 4 x 4 vehicle.

Best months to visit September to December to coincide with the bird-breeding season.

Accommodation Beachfront hotels near Ifaty.

Grading Moderate; the extreme heat can be a problem.

Recommendations At least one night and a very early morning walk are needed to see the rare birds. A local guide is essential. It is easy to get lost.

ANDOHAHELA NATIONAL PARK
Key Species
Mammals Verreaux's sifaka, ring-tailed lemur; otherwise as in Ifaty.

Birds As in Ifaty, but long-tailed ground roller and sub-desert mesite are absent.

Reptiles Numerous species, especally lizards.

Visitor Information
Location 'Parcels' 2 (spiny forest) and 3 (transitional forest) are located to the west of Taolagnaro (Fort Dauphin).

Access There is a good system of marked trails.

Best months to visit September to December, the breeding season.

Accommodation Camping only at Ihazofotsy.

Grading Moderate; the extreme heat can be a problem.

Recommendations Early morning excursions from Berenty are possible. The alternative is to camp for a night. A local guide is essential.

Above 'Spiny forest' near Ifaty. In the foreground is one of the baobabs of the region, *Adansonia rubrostripa*, behind which is *Didiera madagascariensis*.

Left Long-tailed ground roller (*Uratelornis chimera*). This rare endemic bird inhabits only a small area of the southwestern spiny forest.

ISALO NATIONAL PARK

Isalo is quite unlike any other place in Madagascar. Its appeal is the remarkable landscape of eroded 'ruiniforme' sandstone outcrops, canyons, rare plants and the feeling of space. The morning and evening light is often spectacular, making this a special place for photographers. This is Madagascar's most popular national park, and one of the oldest.

Habitat and Terrain

The park covers 81,540ha of the Isalo Massif, which rises from the flat surrounding grassy plain. The sandstone has been eroded into strange shapes, cut through by impressive gorges. Vegetation is concentrated in the canyon bottoms where streams flow. These wooded areas are dominated by the fire-resistant tapia tree (*Uapaca bojeri*), on which a Malagasy endemic silkworm feeds, along with *Pandanus pulcher* and the locally endemic feather palm, *Chrysalidocarpus isaloenses*. On the cliffs and rocks are several endemic succulents including the pachypodium or elephant's foot and the Isalo aloe (*Aloe isaloensis*).

Key Species

Mammals Not prominent, but these may be seen: ring-tailed lemur, Verreaux's sifaka, red-fronted brown lemur.

Birds Benson's rock-thrush, white-throated rail, Madagascar coucal, Madagascar wagtail, Madagascar kestrel, and Madagascar hoopoe.

Reptiles and frogs Oustalet's chameleon, jewel chameleon, spiny-tailed iguanid (*Oplurus quadriomaculatus*), a stump-tailed chameleon, *Brookesia brygooi*, and two locally endemic frogs, the beautifully coloured *Scaphiophryne gottlebei* (see page 101) and the brownish *Mantidactylus corvus*.

Visitor Information

Location Between Fianarantsoa and Toliara (Tuléar) on RN7, to the north of the village of Ranohira.

Access Reached from Ihosy, approximately 90km (2 hours) to the east, or from Toliara 250km to the southwest (3 to 4 hours). A local guide is obligatory if hiking within the park.

Best months to visit Brief rains occur between January and March. Daytime temperatures from June to August are pleasant but nights can be very cold: from November to March days may be too hot. During September and early October the elephant's foot plants are in bloom and temperatures are moderate.

Accommodation Camping only within the park. Reasonable quality hotels in Ranohira and a very comfortable one at the southern edge of the massif.

Grading Moderate (day trips); moderate to difficult if camping and hiking.

Recommendations Even driving through Isalo gives some idea of its rugged beauty. To see any wildlife, however, you must hike and preferably camp. A popular area is the natural swimming pool, La Piscine Naturelle, while for a better chance of lemur-viewing the Canyon des Singes and an extension to the beautiful Grotte de Portugais are worth the effort.

NG

GT

Above Pachypodium rosalatum var. *gracilis* in Isalo National Park.

Left Benson's rock-thrush (*Monticola bensoni*). This rare bird is endemic to Isalo and surrounding area. Its plumage allows it to blend in with the lichen-covered sandstone, but males can often be seen singing in the mornings from prominent rock perches.

37

ANDRINGINTRA NATIONAL PARK

One of Madagascar's newest national parks protects the flora and fauna around its second highest peak, Pic d'Imarivolanitra (2,658m). This is a unique region of granite and gneiss formations, high altitude vegetation, forests and waterfalls, offering some of the best trekking in Madagascar.

Habitat and Terrain
The Andringitra massif and its national park covers 31,160ha. Altitude differences mean that the flora and fauna are very varied, with vegetation ranging from forests to grasslands (with 30 species of terrestrial orchids), and from a spectacular rocky zone to the frosty summit of Pic d'Imarivolanitra: The eastern rainforest and its fauna is virtually inaccessible to tourists at present. Temperatures range from 25°C to –7° C.

Key Species
Mammals Most notable is an ecotype of ring-tailed lemur adapted to high altitudes.

Birds Benson's rock thrush in the high areas.

Reptiles and frogs Little research has been done on the reptiles and frogs.

Visitor Information
Location Between Fianarantsoa and Isalo, 46km south of Ambalavao.

Access There are two entrances: Namoly, 1-hour drive by private vehicle from Ambalavao and Sahanambo Valley at the park's western border, 4 hours from Fianarantsoa. Not accessible by public transport.

Best months to visit The winter months (May to October) are very cold at night but comfortable for walking. Wild flowers are best in the warm, wet season.

Accommodation A comfortable guest house in Ambalamandary; 3 campsites.

Grading Simple accommodation; moderate to strenuous hiking

Recommendations The easiest trail is the beautiful 3-hour hike to the Sacred Waterfall, but the Diavolana trail, a 7-hour circuit, has great views and varied scenery. The trek up Pic d'Imarivolanitra provides the ultimate views.

ZOMBITSE AND VOHIBASIA NATIONAL PARK

This pocket of forest is of major importance to birdwatchers, being home to one of the countries rarest endemics, Appert's greenbul (left). Many other species can be seen in this boundary zone between the western and southern vegetation domains.

Key Species
Mammals and birds Highlights are the pale fork-marked lemur and Coquerel's dwarf lemur. Cuckoo rollers are easy to see here.

Visitor Information
Access From Toliara (2 to 3 hours) or Ranohira (1hour).

Best months to visit October to April.

Grading There is no accommodation. Enthusiastic birders will need to camp.

MAMMALS

Verreaux's sifaka
(Propithecus verreauxi verreauxi)

LEMURS

Lemurs, like ourselves, are primates. Lemurs, however, are regarded as 'primitive' since they share characteristics with early ancestral primates. For this reason they are known as prosimians, or pre-monkeys; other prosimians include the nocturnal bushbabies (galagos), lorises and pottos of Africa and Asia. In contrast to these, many lemur species are active during the day (and periodically during the night) and live in family groups or large troops in which the females are often dominant. This is rare in primates: with most monkeys and great apes the males are larger and indisputably the boss.

Another major difference between the lemurs and their more 'intelligent' monkey relatives is an acute sense of smell, and some species have long, dog-like noses. Scents and smells are important in lemur society and are used extensively for communication, information gathering and marking territories.

By the time the first true primates had evolved, some 70 million years ago, Madagascar had long broken away from Africa and arrived in its current position, so the Mozambique Channel would have presented a formidable obstacle for any animal attempting to cross. Past theories have suggested early primates (and other mammals) may have crossed via a series of now submerged islands or similar 'land bridges', but there is little evidence to support this. The overriding opinion is that, like ancient boat people, lemur-like prosimians arrived on floating rafts of vegetation washed out to sea from mainland Africa. Of course the vast majority of these inadvertent mariners would have perished, but a tiny number completed the voyage successfully and provided the founding stock that subsequently evolved into the variety of lemurs we see today.

We also know that potential lemur competitors and most predators missed the boat, which gave the early prosimian colonists an uninhibited opportunity to diversify and exploit every available niche of this huge island. Lemur diversity is impressive: there are currently no fewer than 53 different varieties (and at least 16 other species are known to have become extinct since man's arrival on the island). They range in size from the tiny pygmy mouse lemur, which could sit in an eggcup, to the indri, a piebald teddy bear weighing around 7kg. One extinct species was larger than a gorilla and weighed about 200kg.

This great diversity (five families and 14 genera) fascinates biologists who marvel that an island this size can hold over a third of the world's primate families. To other visitors the appeal is more fundamental; lemurs are among the most cuddly, endearing and bewitching animals in existence. Their soft fur, round bright eyes and gentle black-gloved hands give them an irresistible appeal.

Lemurs great and small

Left The pygmy mouse lemur (*Microcebus myoxinus*) weighs as little as 25g, and is probably the smallest primate in the world. First named in 1852, it 'disappeared' for over a century through confusion with other species, to be rediscovered and identified in 1994.

Below The indri (*Indri indri*) is arguably the largest lemur and is certainly the most vocal. Indri are easily seen at Andasibe (Périnet) where their haunting song provides one of Madagascar's unforgettable experiences.

THE INDRI FAMILY: INDRIIDAE

The indri family comprises the indri, sifakas (or simponas) and woolly lemurs (or avahis). *Indri indri* live in small family groups in the northeast rainforests, their territories are too big to defend by scent alone, so their song proclaims their whereabouts and warns others to keep away. The sifakas (genus *Propithecus*) are the most widely distributed and diverse members of the family and are real favourites with the majority of visitors.

Indri and sifakas have somewhat human proportions, with long, powerful legs and shorter arms. They are superb leapers, jumping effortlessly from tree to tree, but are awkward on the ground. Whereas visitors seldom see indri descend from their trees, some sifakas frequently need to cross open ground. They bound on their hind legs, bellies thrust out and arms aloft (see opposite), providing observers with one of Madagascar's comic spectacles.

Of the sifaka species, Verreaux's sifaka is the most common. It is divided into four subspecies, two of which are easily seen. *Propithecus verreauxi verreauxi* (page 39, below, and opposite) is one of the main attractions of Berenty, where it feeds on leaves, buds, fruit and flowers. It appears never to drink, and is one of the few mammals at home in the arid Didiereaceae forest where it can leap on to the spiny boughs without damaging its hands or feet.

Below Verreaux's sifaka (*Propithecus verreauxi verreauxi*) sometimes supplement their diet in unusual ways. This female with her infant (the young are born in August and September) is eating a large fungus on the forest floor at Berenty.

JH

Verreaux's sifaka *(Propithecus verreauxi verreauxi)*

NG

Other Sifakas

Coquerel's sifaka (*Propithecus verreauxi coquereli*) is the other commonly seen subspecies. Its chestnut-coloured arms and thighs make it particularly handsome. These sifakas are found in the dry forests of the northwest, and are easy to see in Ampijoroa. The young are born in June and July.

The other two subspecies, the crowned sifaka (*Propithecus verreauxi coronatus*) and Decken's sifaka (*Propithecus verreauxi deckeni*) are confined to more remote areas of western forests and are difficult to see.

Madagascar's eastern forests are the domains of the simpona, *Propithecus diadema*, also divided into four subspecies which are quite dissimilar in appearance. The diademed sifaka (*Propithecus diadema diadema*) is considered by many to be the most beautiful of all the lemurs: its silky coat is a combination of orange, gold, white, silver and black, and it has piercing ruby red eyes. It is also the largest sifaka. Unfortunately it is an elusive animal, but may been seen in Mantadia National Park.

Two other elusive subspecies are *Propithecus diadema candidus*, which is pure white, and *Propithecus diadema perrieri*, which is jet black. Easiest to see (at Ranomafana), however, is *Propithecus diadema edwardsi*, Milne-Edwards' sifaka (see page 21).

The third sifaka species is the golden crowned sifaka (*Propithecus tattersalli*), confined to a tiny enclave of forest near Daraina in the far north.

Woolly Lemurs

The two species of woolly lemur, *Avahi laniger* and *Avahi occidentalis*, are the only nocturnal members of the family, although they are often seen during the day sleeping in trees or shrubs. They may be mistaken for sportive lemurs (*Lepilemur* spp.) until you see the distinctive white patches on the back of the thighs. Woolly lemurs are lethargic animals living on a low-energy diet of – mainly – leaves. Even at night they spend much of their time resting, although in short bursts they can leap speedily through the forest.

Right Eastern woolly lemur (*Avahi laniger*) and her baby in their daytime resting place at Andasibe (Périnet).

CH

Coquerel's sifaka *(Propithecus verreauxi coquereli)*

NG

Diademed sifaka *(Propithecus diadema diadema)*

NG

THE 'TRUE LEMURS': FAMILY LEMURIDAE

These are perhaps the most familiar lemurs, being frequently seen in zoos. The most captivating is surely the ring-tailed lemur (*Lemur catta*), instantly recognisable and synonymous with Madagascar. Ring-tails are the most terrestrial of all lemurs, as visitors to Berenty soon realise when troop members scamper across the sand and surround arriving vehicles. Ring-tails live in troops of around 20 animals in a female-dominant society where scent plays an essential part. Females can be observed rubbing their anal glands against the base of trees; males do the same but also use a spur and gland on their wrists to gouge the bark and enforce the troop's 'keep out' signs. Males also indulge in 'stink fights': after anointing their tails with scent from their wrist glands, they stand glaring at their opponents, their tails quivering aloft like smelly black and white flags.

Ring-tails have a variety of calls, some used to warn of danger (with different calls for aerial and terrestrial dangers). The morning call is like the mewing of a cat (hence the name *catta*). Their varied diet ranges from fruit, leaves and flowers to insects and the occasional reptile. Unlike the sifakas which share their range, they also need to drink so prefer gallery (riverside) forest.

Ring-tailed lemurs are found throughout the southwest of Madagascar. Although Berenty is the easiest place to see them, the neighbouring reserve of Amboasary-Sud is equally rewarding. Isalo, Andringitra and Beza-Mahafaly are other possibilities.

Below Ruffed lemurs. The two subspecies of *Varecia variegata* are uncommon in their eastern rainforest habitat where they are sometimes hunted for food. Black-and-white ruffed lemurs (*Varecia variegata variegata*) are found over quite a large area of north and central eastern rainforest, but the red ruffed lemur (*Varecia variegata rubra*) is confined to the Masoala Peninsula. The Antainambalana River forms a natural barrier between the two subspecies, but in captivity hybrids between the two are quite common.

Twins and sometimes triplets are born in September and October. Baby ruffed lemurs do not cling to their mother but are parked in nests until they are old enough to follow her around the forest canopy.

Varecia variegata variegata

Varecia variegata rubra

MP

HB

GT

Above Ring-tailed lemur (*Lemur catta*). These lemurs generally give birth in August and September, sometimes to twins. Initially the babies cling to the fur of the mother's belly, later riding on her back.

Left This blue-eyed white youngster, nicknamed Sapphire, died before reaching maturity but not before becoming a TV personality. It was not a true albino since it retained the distinctive ringed tail.

Genus *Eulemur*

Widespread throughout the forests of Madagascar, with the exception of spiny forest, the *Eulemur* species share several characteristics. Most noticeably, almost all are sexually dichromatic: males are a different colour from females. Scent also plays an important part in marking territories; females generally spray urine, while males smear secretions from their anal region or heads on to strategic objects – which may include the females. Although more at home in trees, most species spend some time on the ground, strutting about on all fours with their bottoms in the air.

There are five species of *Eulemur*, although some of these are divided into several subspecies. The benchmark (or nominate) species used as the basis to describe the genus is the rather rare mongoose lemur (*Eulemur mongoz*) which can sometimes be seen at Ampijoroa. Mongoose lemurs have interesting behaviour patterns which appear to change with the seasons. During the warm wet months (December to April) they are mainly active during the day (or around dusk), but with the onset of the dry season in May there is a marked shift towards nocturnal activity. This strategy may help them conserve energy when food is less plentiful and also reduce the chance of predation from diurnal birds of prey, when there is little foliage on the trees.

Classification of 'True Lemurs'

Lemur taxonomy (the science of arranging living things into hierarchies of related groups: species, genera, families, etc) has undergone a series of recent revisions. At one time the genus *Lemur* contained all the species now described as *Lemur, Eulemur* and *Varecia*. However, most authorities now regard the ring-tailed lemur (*Lemur catta*) and ruffed lemurs (*Varecia*) as sufficiently different from the others to warrant separation, hence the recent creation of the genus *Eulemur*.

Right Red-bellied lemur, *Eulemur rubriventer*. The white 'tear-drop' patches in front of the eyes show it to be a male. Only males have the rich chestnut-coloured belly which gives it its name. Females have less white on their faces and their chests and underparts are creamy-white. Both sexes have a dark or black tail.

Unusually, these lemurs live in monogamous pairs and both males and females carry the infants on their backs, the males taking over as the youngster becomes heavier.

Above A male crowned lemur (*Eulemur coronatus*). The male's orange-brown coat and black crown are distinctive and contrast with the female (see page 25) which is grey with an orange tiara. Crowned lemurs are only found in the far north of Madagascar, and may be seen in Montagne d'Ambre National Park and Ankarana.

Left Female black lemur (*Eulemur macaco macaco*) in Lokobe Reserve, on the island of Nosy Be. On the nearby island of Nosy Komba, the black lemurs, which are held to be sacred, have never been hunted and so have become tame; this is the most visited wildlife site in Madagsacar. The difference in colour between the sexes is most pronounced in this subspecies: males are all black with bright orange eyes, females are chestnut brown with white ear tufts. The rare, blue-eyed black lemur (*E. m. flavifrons*), which lives in a tiny area of the northwest, has no eartufts and is the only non-human primate with blue eyes.

Brown Lemurs: *Eulemur fulvus*

The brown lemurs are divided into no fewer than six subspecies. In all of these the females are uniform and alike, generally with a brown body and black or grey head, whilst the males show off with a variety of markings, colours and facial hair. These handsome animals not only look different from their mates but from the males of other subspecies. Each subspecies lives in its own distinct range and these join together to form a ring around Madagascar's periphery.

The distribution of the common brown lemur (*E. f. fulvus*) is certainly interesting. It is found in both the central eastern rainforests and the dry deciduous forests of the northwest. When the forest cover on Madagascar was more extensive, it seems likely this lemur was found in the adjoining areas across the central highlands.

The males of two subspecies in particular are notable for their splendid white whiskers. The white-fronted brown lemur (*E. f. albifrons*) (opposite) is the most handsome and is found in the forests of the northeast. Almost as impressive is the male Sanford's brown lemur (*E. f. sanfordi*) which has long cream-coloured eartufts and side-whiskers. The females of both subspecies are a similar uniform brown. However, although both occur in northern Madagascar, their ranges do not overlap so there is little chance of confusion. Sanford's brown lemur is best seen at Montagne d'Ambre National Park and Ankarana, where it shares the forests with the crowned lemur (*Eulemur coronatus*).

Brown lemurs generally live in troops of between five and 15 animals with males and females in roughly equal numbers. Most prefer fruit as the

Right The common brown lemur (*Eulemur fulvus fulvus*). Although hardly 'common' it is readily seen at Ampijoroa and Andasibe (Périnet). Unlike other subspecies, the two sexes are very similar in appearance. Although all brown lemurs are generally considered to be diurnal, many of them are known to be up and about at night as well. The extent of these nocturnal antics may vary with the seasons and is probably also influenced by the cycle of the moon – around full moon they tend to be more active.

White-fronted brown lemur (*Eulemur fulvus albifrons*). The male, with his snowy-white head and creamy underparts, is gorgeous; the female (*left*) is less impressive. Nosy Mangabe is the best place to see them in the wild, but an easy option is to visit the free-range troop at Ivoloina Zoo, near Toamasina (Tamatave).

Top Male red-fronted brown lemur (*Eulemur fulvus rufus*). This is the brown lemur most commonly seen by visitors – it occurs in the southeast (Ranomafana) and the west (Kirindy) but the best opportunity for a close view is at Berenty where it has been introduced. Males can be recognised by their greyish coat with a rufous crown, whilst females are pale chestnut brown with a grey crown. Both sexes have conspicuous white patches above their eyes and long dark noses.

Above Male collared lemur (*Eulemur fulvus collaris*). This subspecies was also introduced to Berenty where it was much less successful than *E. f. rufus*. It has now disappeared from Berenty but may be seen in Andohahela.

mainstay of their diet, along with leaves and flowers. However, at Ranomafana National Park, the red-fronted brown lemur (*E. f. rufus*) has been observed eating giant millipedes, first wiping off any unpleasant secretions with its tail, before tucking into the unlikely snack.

BAMBOO OR GENTLE LEMURS

The genus *Hapalemur* are commonly known as the bamboo lemurs, and for good reason, as these endearing animals are the Malagasy equivalent of giant pandas: bamboo and similar vegetation make up most of their diet. They are also less commonly referred to as gentle lemurs. There are three species.

The most widespread is the grey bamboo lemur (*Hapalemur griseus*) which occurs as three subspecies. The eastern grey bamboo lemur (*H. g. griseus*) is found throughout the rainforest belt – often close to roads or paths and by the forest edge where bamboo thickets flourish. Although far less abundant, bamboo does grow in some areas of deciduous forest in the west, but the western grey bamboo lemur (*H. g. occidentalis*) is rarely seen. The third subspecies, the Lac Alaotra reed lemur (*H. g. alaotrensis*), is unique amongst primates in that it lives above water in the reed beds on which it feeds. Lac Alaotra is a major rice-growing centre and is gradually being drained and the reeds cleared. These activities have caused a catastrophic decline in the reed lemur population – perhaps as few as 7,000 survive.

Above The eastern grey bamboo lemur (*Hapalemur griseus griseus*) is the most widespread of the bamboo lemurs.

Left The Lac Alaotra reed lemur (*Hapalemur griseus alaotrensis*) is perhaps the most restricted of the *Hapalemur* genus. This critically endangered lemur is restricted to a small area of Lac Alaotra.

53

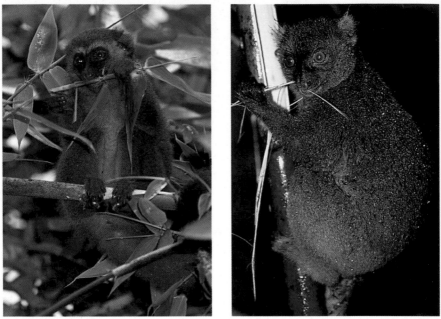

Golden bamboo lemur.   Greater bamboo lemur.

The two other species of *Hapalemur*, the golden bamboo lemur (*Hapalemur aureus*) and the greater bamboo lemur (*Hapalemur simus*) are also highly endangered. The golden bamboo lemur was not discovered until 1985 and became the catalyst for the creation of Ranomafana National Park which, for several years, was its only known home. Recently, however, populations have been discovered in Andringitra National Park.

Golden bamboo lemurs have a particular preference for the leaf bases and new shoots of giant bamboo which, while being rich in protein, are also laced with levels of cyanide toxin that would be lethal to other animals. This species is generally seen in groups of three or four, most often an adult male and female, with sub-adults and offspring. Interestingly, recent research suggests that, unlike other lemur social hierarchies, the males may be dominant.

By far the largest member of this group is the greater bamboo lemur, which at around 2kg is twice the weight of the other species. Although subfossil evidence indicates this lemur was once widespread in rainforest areas, it is today restricted to areas around Ranomafana, Andringitra and Vondrozo. In common with the golden bamboo lemur, this species has a particular liking for giant bamboo; however, to avoid competition with its congener, the greater bamboo lemur feeds almost exclusively on the inner pith. Using its large teeth and strong jaws, it is able to break through the tough bamboo pole and strip away the outer layers to reach the pith beneath. This is highly destructive and ravaged stands of giant bamboo are clear evidence of the presence of this lemur.

NOCTURNAL LEMURS

Grey mouse lemur (Microcebus murinus)

THE MOUSE LEMURS AND DWARF LEMURS: FAMILY CHEIROGALEIDAE

Mouse Lemurs (genus *Microcebus*)

Madagascar's tiny, and very lively, mouse lemurs are the most abundant of the island's primates. The grey mouse lemur, *Microcebus murinus* (see page 55), lives in the drier forests of the south and west, while the brown mouse lemur, *Microcebus rufus* (see page 124), prefers the wetter east. The pygmy mouse lemur, *Microcebus myoxinus* (see page 41), has so far only been observed in Kirindy and the nearby reserve of Analabe. As recently as 1998 a fourth species was discovered. The golden-brown mouse lemur (*Microcebus ravelobensis*) is only known from the forests around Lac Ravelobe (from which it takes its name) at Ampijoroa in the northwest.

Dwarf Lemurs (genus *Cheirogaleus*)

There are two species: the greater dwarf lemur (*Cheirogaleus major*), which lives in the east, and the fat-tailed dwarf lemur (*Cheirogaleus medius*), which is found in the west and south. The easier one to see is *C. major* which, in the warm season, is common along the roadside near Andasibe (Périnet) and Ranomafana. During the cold winter months dwarf lemurs aestivate (ie hibernate), living off the fat in their tails, a unique feature among primates. Even when active they are slow moving, particularly in contrast with the scampering mouse lemurs.

Other Family Members (genera *Mirza*, *Phaner* and *Allocebus*)

The remaining members of the family are represented by Coquerel's dwarf lemur (*Mirza coquereli*), the fork-marked lemur (*Phaner furcifer*) and the hairy-eared dwarf lemur (*Allocebus trichotis*). Coquerel's dwarf lemur lives in the dry western forests and behaves like a mouse lemur but is much larger. The four subspecies of fork-marked lemur are distributed in the forests of both the east and west. They can be identified by the black line along the back, which forks at the head, ending at each eye.

WEASEL OR SPORTIVE LEMURS: FAMILY MEGALADAPIDAE

The generic name, *Lepilemur*, is more appropriate for general use than the choice of vernacular names: lepilemurs don't look like weasels and are not very sportive. They are most often seen during the day, peering dozily out of their sleeping holes in tree trunks or, where there no holes, from a fork in the branches. At night, however, they are often very vocal and active.

Despite their small size, lepilemurs are related to some of the large extinct lemurs from the genus *Megaladapis*, although they differ enough to warrant their own subfamily, Lepilemurinae.

Nine species are known, their ranges forming an almost continuous ring around Madagascar. Many are very similar in appearance so geographical location is usually the most reliable means of identification.

Top Greater dwarf lemur
(*Cheirogaleus major*), Mantadia.

Above left Northern sportive lemur
(*Lepilemur septentrionalis*), Ankarana.

Above right White-footed sportive lemur
(*Lepilemur leucopus*), Berenty.

Left Red-tailed sportive lemur
(*Lepilemur ruficaudatus*), Kirindy.

AYE-AYE: FAMILY DAUBENTONIIDAE

There is only one member of this family, the aye-aye (*Daubentonia madagascariensis*). This is a seriously weird animal which was only classified as a lemur in relatively recent times: originally scientists took it to be a squirrel-like rodent. What makes it so unusual? It has a disproportionately long and bushy tail; it has teeth like a rodent – they never stop growing; its ears are like those of a bat – but even larger and more mobile – and so sensitive that it can apparently hear a grub moving under the bark of a tree; it has claws not fingernails (except on the great toe); it has inguinal teats (between its back legs not on its chest); it has no fixed mating season but can give birth at any time of the year. And it has that extraordinary finger.

Most descriptions of the aye-aye say that the middle finger is 'greatly elongated'. In fact it is no longer than the middle finger of other primates, including man. But it is extraordinarily thin, skeletal in fact, and this makes it look longer. The aye-aye also keeps the other fingers crooked up out of the way when working with its most important digit, so its hand looks like a tarantula spider. The thin finger is designed to fit through the gnawed holes in tree branches or large nuts (coconuts are now a favourite) and winkle out the tasty contents, while all the time the aye-aye's ears move to pick up the slightest sound.

If you can't see an aye-aye in the wild, try to see one in a zoo (Tsimbazaza in Antananarivo, or in Jersey, London, Paris or Duke University Primate Center, USA). However, aye-ayes seem to be popping up all over Madagascar, and the chances of seeing one in the wild are improving. Nosy Mangabe (see page 16) is still the best place, or on Aye-Aye Island in Mananara, but very occasionally they have been seen by the road at Andasibe (Périnet).

Left The aye-aye using its thin middle finger to extract grubs from a tree cavity.

Aye-aye *(Daubentonia madagascariensis)*

MP

CARNIVORES: THE CIVETS AND MONGOOSES

CARNIVORE CONFUSION

There are only eight species of native carnivore in Madagascar (a low number compared with other mammal groups); all are endemic and are split between two families, the civets and their allies (Viverridae) and the mongooses (Herpestidae). These animals share certain basic characteristics with civets and mongooses on mainland Africa, but there are also considerable differences; strong evidence that the evolutionary pathways of Africa and Madagascar diverged a long time ago.

There are three civet-like carnivores: the fosa (*Cryptoprocta ferox*) belonging to its own subfamily, Cryptoproctinae, and the fanaloka or striped civet (*Fossa fossana*) and falanouc (*Eupleres goudotii*) which comprise the subfamily Euplerinae.

The common names for these animals are very confusing. *Fossa fossana*, the striped civet, is often confused with fosa (*Cryptoprocta ferox*). Presumably, this mistake was first made by Gray in 1865 when he gave the civet its generic name, *Fossa*. To add to the muddle, the striped civet's Malagasy name, fanaloka is pronounced 'fanalook' and causes inevitable confusion with the falanouc (*Eupleres goudotii*). Further, the Malagasy themselves often use fosa or fossa (pronounced foosa, with the 'a' almost silent) as a general term that may refer to a number of the island's carnivores, depending on the region of Madagascar. We will be consistent and use fosa, fanaloka and falanouc.

Left A female falanouc (*Eupleres goudotii*) with her young.

Above Fanaloka or Malagasy striped civet (*Fossa fossana*). This cat-sized animal, found mainly in the eastern rainforests, is shy and strictly nocturnal. However, there is an excellent chance of seeing it at Ranomafana.

Left Fosa (*Cryptoprocta ferox*). The fosa is Madagascar's largest carnivore, measuring about 2m in length, half of which is tail which it uses for balance. It is an expert climber and the main predator of lemurs. This photo shows the pads and retractile, curved claws which enable it to pursue its prey up trees. Fosas are rarely seen by visitors, being secretive and mainly nocturnal. The best place to see them is Kirindy.

CIVET-LIKE CARNIVORES

The fosa resembles an elongated, short-legged puma (when first discovered it was thought to be a member of the cat family), although its general build is much more slender: it rarely weighs more than 10kg. It is at home in the trees and on the ground and, outside the breeding season, is solitary. Females have, in effect, a false penis: the clitoris is elongated and has a central bone. Mating is prolonged and noisy!

The fanaloka or Malagasy striped civet is a small, spotted, fox-like carnivore the size of a domestic cat. Fanalokas live in pairs in the eastern rainforests, foraging for food in the dense undergrowth. In preparation for the leaner winter months, they are able to lay down fat reserves, especially in the tail.

Madagascar's most specialised carnivore is the falanouc. This uncommon and secretive animal lives in the lowland rainforests of the east and northeast. It is larger than the fanaloka and has an extended snout and tiny teeth – features that help it catch the earthworms and other invertebrates which are its exclusive diet. The claws and forepaws are well developed for digging and are also used for defence. The falanouc gives birth to extremely well-developed young: babies are born with their eyes open and are able to follow their mother and hide in vegetation within two days.

MONGOOSES

Madagascar's mongooses, of which there are five species, all belong to the endemic subfamily Galidiinae. The commonest and most widespread species is the ring-tailed mongoose (*Galidia elegans*), which is split into three subspecies which inhabit different forest regions. All have a rich russet coat and distinctive banded tail. They are sociable creatures, often found in vocal family groups. Equally at home on the ground or in the branches of trees, they forage for rodents, young birds, eggs, reptiles and invertebrates.

The narrow-striped mongoose (*Mungotictus decemlineata*) is found only in the dry areas of the west. These delightful grey/sandy coloured animals have several faint dark stripes along their flanks and back and a large bushy tail which is held erect when alarmed.

The little-studied brown-tailed mongoose (*Salanoia concolor*) lives in the northeastern rainforests. It is known to be active mainly during the day and to feed mostly on insects.

The broad-striped mongoose (*Galidictis fasciata*), of the eastern rainforests, is the most specialised flesheater in the subfamily. It is mainly nocturnal, feeding on rodents, lizards and frogs. Its cousin, the Grandidier's mongoose (*Galidictis grandidieri*) was only discovered in 1986, after the examination of mislabelled museum specimens. It is the largest and least known mongoose species, and may be restricted to the spiny forest areas around Lac Tsimanampetsotsa in the southwest.

Above Northern ring-tailed mongoose (*Galidia elegans dambrensis*). These pretty animals often visit the campsites in reserves such as Ankarana.

Below Narrow-striped mongoose (*Mungotictus decemlineata*). Locally called 'boky-boky', this mongoose is limited to the dry western forests, particularly Kirindy.

TENRECS

Tenrecs (family Tenrecidae) are insectivores, a group of mammals which have flourished in Madagascar, branching into at least 27 species. Tenrecs are divided into two sub-families: Tenrecinae, the so-called 'spiny tenrecs' (five species), and Oryzoryctinae, the furred tenrecs, with about 22 species.

Not all the 'spiny' tenrecs live up to their name. The largest, the tail-less or common tenrec (*Tenrec ecaudatus*), has only a few spines hidden in its fur. It weighs up to 2kg and is a popular source of meat for the Malagasy (see page 102). The reproductive capabilities of the common tenrec are remarkable: it can produce up to 32 embryos at one time and has 24 nipples. Not all the babies survive, but those that do follow their mother around the forest in orderly columns, wearing stripy, spiny coats for camouflage and defence.

The greater hedgehog tenrec (*Setifer setosus*) and lesser hedgehog tenrec (*Echinops telfairi*) look very much like hedgehogs, and also roll themselves into a prickly ball. The former is found in both western and eastern forests, while the latter is restricted to the drier regions of the southwest.

In the rainforest areas, the most commonly encountered species are the streaked tenrecs: *Hemicentetes semispinosus* from the lowlands, and *H. nigriceps* from the highlands. Both have sharp yellow spines mixed in with softer black prickles arranged in longitudinal stripes, and orange-yellow underparts. A specialised set of dorsal spines is used for communication: they can be vibrated together to produce a threatening rattle (called stridulation) or an inaudible (to humans) sound used to call straying youngsters or family members.

The 'furred' tenrecs have evolved to fill niches occupied elsewhere by shrews, moles or desmans. There are probably more than 17 species of shrew tenrec (genus *Microgale*), which can sometimes only be distinguished from each other by close examination of their teeth! By far the most interesting and remarkable member of this subfamily is the very rare aquatic tenrec (*Limnogale mergulus*), which has developed webbed feet and a flattened tail for swimming. It lives in fast-flowing streams, where it forages for frogs, fish, crustaceans and aquatic insect larvae.

Aquatic tenrec (*Limnogale mergulus*).

Above left Highland streaked tenrec (*Hemicentetes nigriceps*). These little yellow and black striped tenrecs are found at high altitudes such as Andringitra. Their relative, the lowland streaked tenrec (*H. semispinosus*), is more often seen, foraging for earthworms in eastern forests or by the roadside. The formidable cream-coloured spines are used for head-butting attackers.

Above right Large-eared tenrec (*Geogale aurita*). This mouse-like inhabitant of the western forests uses its keen hearing to locate termites in rotting trees. Like other tenrecs it may aestivate (go into a torpor) during the dry months when food is scarce.

Below Greater hedgehog tenrec (*Setifer setosus*). This widespread species forages on the forest floor while the lesser hedghog tenrec (*Echinops telfairi*), which is confined to the dry forests of the south, is, surprisingly, an agile tree climber. It aestivates during the dry season.

RODENTS

Madagascar has around 22 native rodent species, all of which belong to the endemic subfamily Nesomyinae. The most celebrated is the giant jumping rat (*Hypogeomys antimena*) which is restricted to a small area in the west (see page 29). This charming animal is the size of a rabbit and fills a similar ecological niche: it lives in family groups and digs a network of burrows.

Perhaps the easiest species to see is the red forest rat (*Nesomys rufus*), which may be active during the day and is common in many rainforest areas, particularly Ranomafana.

Nocturnal white-tailed tree rats (genus *Brachytarsomys*) of which there are two species, also inhabit rainforest areas and are unusual in being totally tree-dwelling. They have developed prehensile tails for gripping branches. There are perhaps as many as 12 different species of tuft-tailed rat (genus *Eliurus*), which are also arboreal, but have tails that end in a conspicuous brush-like tuft. Vole rats (genus *Brachyuromys*) construct networks of runways beneath thick tangles of vegetation and matted grasses.

The smallest of the island's rodents are the big-footed mice from the genus *Macrotarsomys*. These species are confined to the drier forests and grasslands of the west.

Below left The inquisitive red forest rat (*Nesomys rufus*) is often seen around campsites.

Below right Macrotarsomys bastardi, a gerbil-like mouse from the western forests.

QB

QB

BATS

Bats (order Chiroptera) are split into two very distinct groups: the fruit bats, and flying foxes (Megachiroptera), and the insectivorous-type bats (Microchiroptera). Both these groups are represented in Madagascar, although they are the least studied of the island's mammals. Given the relative ease with which bats can travel over long distances (and more importantly over water), it is hardly surprising that there are fewer endemic species of bats here than in the other groups of mammals.

There are three species of fruit bat, of which the Madagascar flying fox (*Pteropus rufus*) is the largest – its wingspan may reach 1.5m and it can weigh over 1kg. The name flying fox is appropriate – they do indeed look like little foxes, with long muzzles and very mobile ears. They are generally found in large colonies in forests and often on islands around the coast where there is a small patch of forest.

The second largest species is the straw-coloured fruit bat (*Eidolon dupreanum*) which is widespread but patchily distributed around the island. It is the only fruit bat known to occur on the high plateau. In contrast, the third fruit bat species, the Madagascar rousette (*Rousettus madagascariensis*) is found mainly in rainforest areas, but also in some deciduous forests in the west. It prefers to roost in caves (and not trees like other fruit bats); indeed

Above The Madagascar flying fox (*Pteropus rufus*) is a familiar sight in some areas. Noisy colonies congregate in favourite roost trees in reserves such as Berenty, and on islands like Nosy Tanikely (*right*). They are often active during the day, taking off en masse to circle their roost before hanging upside down from a branch. This bat has relatives on other Indian Ocean islands, but otherwise its nearest family members are in Asia – there are no *Pteropus* species in Africa.

it only occurs in areas where caves are present and may posses some rudimentary echolocation capabilities to aid navigation in low light.

Six families from the suborder Microchiroptera are represented in Madagascar (there are 19 worldwide), although only one of these, Myzopodidae, is endemic. It contains a single species, the sucker-footed bat (*Myzopoda aurita*). This rare bat is found in the eastern rainforest and derives its name from peculiar suction discs on the wrists and feet, which help the animal to hang from the smooth leaves of palms, where it likes to roost.

Although known as 'insectivorous-type' bats, by no means all Microchiroptera eat insects. As more research takes places in Madagascar the number of species will, no doubt, be added to. To date 20 or so have been described, many of which also occur on mainland Africa.

The best place to see several species of bat is Ankarana, with its many caves.

Below left Madagascar red trident bat (*Triaenops persicus rufus*). This endemic subspecies of leaf-nosed bat has three 'prongs' above the 'nose leaf' instead of the more usual one. The prongs and 'leaf' are part of the bat's echolocation system, an extraordinarily complex means of navigation used by many bats which is still imperfectly understood. Possibly the prongs act as a sound splitter, directing the echo of the bat's squeaks – or sounds made by its prey – into stereophonic sound to give better direction finding. The 'leaf' and ears act together to ensure that both prey-detection and navigation can take place simultaneously.

Below right Madagascar mouse-eared bat (*Myotis goudoti*). This bat does not have a leaf-nose, but in front of each ear is a projection or tragus, which may have an equivalent function to the nose prong in leaf-nosed bats. This bat is endemic to Madagascar and the unusual russet colour on the upper parts possibly affords some camouflage on the so-called 'red island'.

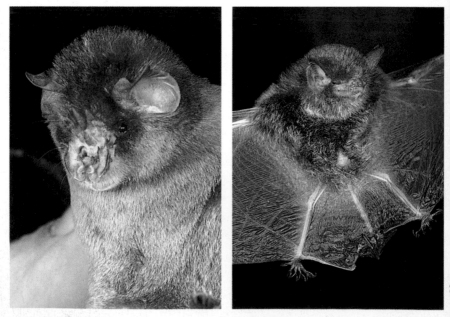

BIRDS

Pitta-like ground roller *(Aterlornis pittoides)*

ENDEMIC ODDITIES

Madagascar has only about 283 bird species, but is home to 37 endemic genera – more than any other country in the African region. Here it is quality not quantity that attracts birders. There are 109 endemic species (51% of the 209 breeding species) with five endemic families and one endemic subfamily. The vast majority are more or less dependent on the native forests or wetlands and very few inhabit the more open central highlands.

Madagascar shares 20 species with either the Comoros or Seychelles. Many of these belong to genera confined to various western Indian Ocean islands, such as the vasa parrots, blue pigeons, and the fodys. Happily it is the species present on Madagascar which are plentiful, in contrast to their endangered cousins on the other islands.

The beautiful bird on page 69 is the pitta-like ground roller (*Aterlornis pittoides*). The ground rollers (Brachypteraciidae) are a most attractive family. There are four rainforest species including the pitta-like ground roller and scaly ground roller (see page 15) and one from the spiny forest, the long-tailed ground roller (see page 35). Most excavate long nest burrows. The short-legged ground roller, however, nests in tree cavities up to 20m above ground.

There are ten handsome coua species and some are easy to see. Couas are related to cuckoos and coucals but are sufficiently distinct to warrant

Identifying birds can seem a daunting business, so here are two endemic species that are unmistakable:
Left The crested drongo (*Dicrurus forficatus*), is black with a deeply forked tail and comical 'crest'.
Below The Madagascar red fody (*Foudia madagascariensis*), one of four endemic weavers, dresses to impress the ladies, so outside the breeding season (November to April) is a boring brownish colour.

NG

OLIBIOS

Left Crested coua (*Coua cristata*). The most widely spread coua, it is found mainly in western dry forests but it is also present in the eastern rainforests.

their own subfamily, Couinae. Despite being largely forest birds, only three magpie-size species are arboreal: the blue coua from rainforests, and the crested coua and Verreaux's coua (*Coua verreauxi*) which are mainly found in drier areas. These birds bear a striking resemblance to Africa's touracos. All couas share two conspicuous characteristics: featherless, blue skin around the eyes and long, broad tails. The six ground-dwelling species behave in a similar manner to the American roadrunner or the Old World pheasants. The largest is the rather stately giant coua (*Coua gigas*), shown on page 33, which is often heard before it is seen. The running coua (*Coua cursor*) may be encountered sprinting through the spiny forest. It has an area of black skin on the rump which it exposes to the rays of the early morning sun after a particularly cold night. The red-capped coua (*Coua ruficeps*) and Coquerel's coua (*Coua coquereli*), which inhabit the western and southern areas, also warm themselves in this way. The red-fronted coua (*Coua reynaudii*) and red-breasted coua (*Coua serriana*) are both rainforest birds.

Above Blue coua (*Coua caerula*). This bird of the rainforest may also occasionally be seen in Ankarana.

Primitive Parrots

To the uninitiated, Madagascar's black vasa parrots (*Coracopsis* spp.) hardly merit a second glance. But these drab-looking birds have unbelievably exotic love lives. Unlike the respectable monogamous parrots in other parts of the world, greater vasa parrots are promiscuously polygamous, with the larger female taking the initiative in courtship. The males have risen to the challenge by evolving a penis (actually an outpocketing of the cloaca) the size of a golf ball; mating takes a couple of hours with vasa onlookers enjoying the spectacle!

The Birds and the Beaks

The vangas (Vangidae) are undoubtedly the most celebrated endemic bird family in Madagascar. Had Charles Darwin sailed to this island instead of the Galapagos, and seen vangas instead of finches, his thoughts on species and evolution would surely have been similarly provoked. Such is the diversity in size, colour and in particular beak shape of the various species that it is hard to imagine they are related at all. Yet characteristics of the skull and other structural features confirm a common ancestry similar to the helmet shrikes of Africa. Today they fill niches that are occupied in other parts of the world by woodpeckers, woodhoopoes, shrikes, tits, treecreepers and nuthatches – all birds absent from Madagascar. Most vangas are gregarious and often seen in mixed feeding flocks.

The size and shape of the various vanga beaks reflect the size of their insect prey, its location and the mode of capture. Larger species, like the hook-billed vanga, have a robust beak with a characteristic hook at the tip to help them deal with their carnivorous diet of large insects, chameleons and other small vertebrates. The extraordinary helmet vanga (see page 13 and opposite) comes into this category. Members of the *Xenopirostris* genus, such as Pollen's vanga, use their laterally compressed beaks to rip bark from dead wood. The more lightly built Chabert's vanga behaves like a flycatcher, grabbing insects on the wing.

The sickle-billed vanga is the largest and most easily identifiable species. Its babbling, cackling call, gregariousness and feeding behaviour are similar to Africa's woodhoopoes. It lives in the western forests where its bill is used for probing crevices in the bark of trees.

The smaller species, which include the red-tailed vanga (*Calicalicus madagascariensis*), nuthatch vanga (*Hypositta corallirostris*) and recently described red-shouldered vanga (*Calicalicus rufocarpalis*), have much finer beaks suited to hunting out small insects along branches and tree trunks.

Recent investigations have revealed that the Crossley's babbler (*Mystacornis crossleyi*) and the Ward's flycatcher (*Pseudobias wardi*) are in fact also vangas. Formerly grouped with the two Oxylabes, the Crossley's babbler is therefore the only terrestrial vanga, while the Ward's flycatcher tends to hawk insects, as its name would imply. Studies are also currently being conducted on the four diminutive Newtonias, which may yet be added to the vangas.

Above left Chabert's vanga
(*Leptopterus chaberti*).

Centre left Pollen's vanga (*Xenopirostris polleni*).

Below left Blue vanga
(*Cyanolanius madagascariensis*).

Above right Hook-billed vanga
(*Vanga curvirostris*).

Centre right Sickle-billed vanga
(*Falculea palliata*).

Below right Helmet vanga (*Euryceros prevostii*).

DH/BIOS

Above Brown mesite (*Mesitornis unicolor*). The mesites (Mesitornithidae) are a peculiar family of ground-dwelling birds that rarely fly even when pursued by predators. Instead they freeze, relying on their cryptic colouring to help them blend into the background. There are only three species: the brown mesite, found in the eastern rainforest, the white-breasted mesite (*Mesitornis variegata*), a deciduous forest bird, and the subdesert mesite (*Monias benschi*) from the spiny forest.

Right (above and below) The asity family (Philepittidae) shows striking differences between males and females. In breeding plumage, the males of all four species sport iridescent blue-green wattles, caruncles and naked areas of facial skin.

OL/BIOS

Above right Male sunbird asity (*Neodrepanis coruscans*) from the smallest of the two genera. The sunbird asity's close resemblance to true sunbirds illustrates the principle of convergent evolution: if a design works, repeat it.

Below right Male velvet asity *(Philepitta castanea)*. These lovely birds, found in the eastern rainforest, are sometimes seen in Périnet and (more often) at Ranomafana.

GT

RARITIES AND REDISCOVERIES

Madagascar red owl (*Tyto soumagnei*)

BACK FROM THE BRINK?

Until very recently several of Madagascar's endemic birds were considered to be on the brink of extinction or extinct – sadly true of the Alaotra little grebe (*Tachybaptus rufolavatus*) and Madagascar pochard (*Aythya innotata*). But the recent surge of interest in Madagascar and dramatic increase in research has revealed a number of pleasant surprises.

The two most celebrated examples are the Madagascar serpent eagle (*Eutriorchis astur*) and Madagascar red owl (*Tyto soumagnei*) (see page 75). The serpent eagle had eluded conclusive detection for 50 years until a dead specimen found in the rain forests of Ambatovaky confirmed its existence. Since then live specimens have been captured on the Masoala peninsula and seen at other locations. Similarly, the red owl had not been seen since 1973 until its rediscovery near Andapa in the mid 1990s. Rather than teetering on the brink of extinction, these species have emerged from obscurity having been overlooked because of their secretive nature.

The marsh-dwelling Sakalava rail (*Amaurornis olivieri*), not seen for 33 years until its 1995 rediscovery at Lac Bemamba in the west, is now known to have a small breeding population in the Mahavavy Delta wetlands. Lac Bemamba is also one of the last haunts of the Madagascar or Bernier's teal (*Anas bernieri*), which is the westernmost species of a cluster of grey teals with Australasian affinities. Both these species have suffered calamitous declines due to the draining and loss of their wetland habitats for conversion to rice paddies and through hunting.

Another crake thought to be on the verge of extinction was the slender-billed flufftail, but thorough surveys of a number of upland marsh areas adjacent to rainforest have revealed several isolated populations.

Despite continuing loss of habitat, new bird species are still being found in Madagascar. Two completely new names have recently been added to the ornithological register. Prior to its description in 1995, the cryptic warbler (*Cryptosylvicola randrianasoloi*) had simply not been recognised for what it was and had been regularly dismissed as one of the jery species. It was largely differences in its call that alerted ornithologists to it being something new and now it has been located in many rainforest areas. More recently, the red-shouldered vanga (*Calicalicus rufocarpalis*) has been identified from areas of *Euphorbia* scrub south of Toliara (Tuléar). It closely resembles the more common and widespread red-tailed vanga (*Calicalicus madagascariensis*), but their respective ranges do not overlap.

In addition new species have come into being through the reclassification of known birds. This is the result of scientists looking more closely at different populations of a species and deciding that separation of these populations is valid. There have been three such cases recently; the sub-desert brush warbler (*Nesillas lantzii*) from spiny forests areas, Amber Mountain rock thrush (*Monticola erythronotus*) from Mt d'Ambre and the torotoroka scops owl (*Otus madagascariensis*) from the drier areas of the west and south.

REPTILES
AND FROGS

Boettger's chameleon *(Calumma boettgeri)*

REPTILES

Madagascar is a wonderful place for herpetologists (people who study reptiles and amphibians), with around 340 known reptile species and more being added almost every month as new surveys are done. Over 90% are endemic.

Although you would expect Madagascar to share most of its reptile families with Africa, many well-known ones from the mainland are absent. For instance, among lizards there are no agamas, no 'typical' lizards of the Lacertidae family, and no monitors. On land there are no front-fanged venomous snakes (which means, in effect, there are none of the deadly species such as vipers, cobras and mambas) and no pythons. In fact, some families have their closest relatives in South America: the iguanid lizards and the boas.

CHAMELEONS: FAMILY CHAMAELEONIDAE

Chameleons are mostly found in Africa and Madagascar. About half the world's chameleons are unique to Madagascar – currently 67 species have been identified – and new ones are still being discovered.

Chameleons are perhaps the most distinctive and specialised of all lizards, perfectly designed for life in the trees. Evolution has done an exquisite job here, modifying almost every bodily feature (the *Brookesia* genus is the exception – see pages 84, 85 and 131). A chameleon's body is laterally flattened, enabling the animal to move easily through tangles of branches and allowing them to absorb heat efficiently in the morning and evening by turning broadside to the sun. This shape provides an imposing profile to deter predators and other chameleons (they are all strictly solitary). An angry or frightened chameleon puffs itself up to look even bigger. This ability to inflate themselves with air provides an effective flotation device – chameleons are good swimmers.

It is the chameleon's eyes that most people notice first. Large, and protected by circular eyelids which cover all but the pupils, they can be swivelled independently so the reptile can look in two directions at once without needing to move its head. This is extremely useful for an animal that relies on camouflage to avoid predation: it can keep absolutely still but watch out for danger – and food – in all directions. When food is located (usually an insect), both eyes point forward. The chameleon can then judge depth and distance and bring into action its most specialised feature – its tongue. This rests like a primed missile in the chameleon's mouth before being fired at potential prey. The tongue can extend to a length equal to the animal's body, and if the aim is good a sticky muscular tip clamps onto the victim and seals its fate.

NG

NG

Perfect adaptation to life in the trees

Above left Warty chameleon (*Furcifer verrucosus*). Using its prehensile tail as a fifth hand, the chameleon is an agile climber. Chameleons seem to prefer to rest on thin branches; perhaps they are safer from heavier predators, although exposed to a passing bird – or human.

Above right Female Parson's chameleon (*Calumma parsonii*). A chameleon's toes and fingers are fused together in two opposing groups like a pair of pliers – an ideal adaptation for gripping branches. The independently moving eyes can be seen here: one eye keeps the photographer in view and the other watches where the chameleon is going.

Below Panther chameleon (*Furcifer pardalis*). The speed with which the tongue shoots out to hit its target has been measured at less than a quarter of a second.

Goliaths and midgets

The world's largest and smallest chameleons. Two species compete for the heavyweight title: Oustalet's chameleon (*Furcifer oustaleti*), *top*, from the drier areas of the west and southwest, and Parson's chameleon (*Calumma parsonii*), *centre*, which lives in the eastern rainforests, where four forms are recognised. Both these giants can exceed 60cm in length (including the tail). Oustalet's chameleon varies a lot in colour; many are a dull shade of grey-brown.

The nose-horned chameleon (*Calumma nasuta*), *below*, is the smallest of the 'typical' chameleons. Its total length rarely exceeds 100mm, and much of that is tail. However, the most minuscule chameleon of all is a pygmy stump-tailed chameleon (*Brookesia minima*), *centre*, which is barely longer than a fingernail, 35mm in total length.

A Coat of Many Colours

Chameleons do not change colour to match their background! It is just one of the several beliefs that have been attached to this extraordinary lizard through the centuries. In ancient times they were probably kept as pets in southern Europe: Aristotle described their ability to change colour and Shakespeare and his contemporaries claimed they fed on air (the caged chameleons presumably caught insects that came within tongue-shot).

In the chameleon's world, colour is a language used to defend territories, convey emotions and communicate with potential mates. It is also a means of regulating body temperature. The way the change in colour is achieved is fascinating. Cells containing a variety of pigments lie underneath the skin and are able to 'open' and 'close' to expose their pigment. Colour change is controlled by a combination of hormonal and nervous activity. For instance, a distressed or angry chameleon opens cells containing the brown pigment, melanin, which turns it much darker. When the chameleon relaxes, yellow cells and blue cells combine, resulting in the calmer, more normal shades of green. Sexual excitement produces an explosion of colours and patterns. At night many chameleons turn almost white, perhaps the result of total relaxation.

Above A panther chameleon crossing the road gives lie to the belief that chameleons change colour to match their background. This male is in the breeding colours that he adopts during the wet season when mating and egg-laying take place. Females, which, in this species, are a pinkish-brown colour, need soft, moist soil to dig holes for their eggs. Chameleons are awkward on the ground and adopt a swaying motion which perhaps makes them less conspicuous to a normal predator, but enables human admirers to catch them with ease.

Right A defensive female Labord's chameleon (*Furcifer labordi*) in Kirindy. This chameleon is putting on the works: she is already in her breeding colours, which have intensified under stress. In addition, she inflates herself with air, dilates her throat, and opens her mouth to show its bright orange interior.

A Nose for all Occasions

Anything Cyrano or Pinocchio could do, chameleons can do better. The array of weird and wonderful noses displayed by Madagascar's chameleons is fantastic, from small rounded bumps to twin prongs and long slender lances. Although often called 'horns', they are in fact scale-covered extensions of the nose, and are known scientifically as rostral protuberances. Generally only the males have them: they are used, like colour, in combat and to impress the females.

Noses are useful for others of the same species, especially when related species live in close proximity to one another. Experiments have shown that, if the protuberances are removed, the individual chameleon can be thrown into total confusion and is not recognised by its own kind.

Below A courting panther chameleon (*Furcifer pardalis*) shows off his range of seductive colours (compare with his 'normal' colouring on page 81).

BL

Furcifer willsii

Calumma malthe

Calumma boettgeri

Furcifer rhinoceratus

Furcifer antimena

Furcifer bifidus

Furcifer minor

Calumma parsonii

Chameleons in Miniature

The stump-tailed or leaf chameleons from the genus *Brookesia* are the most diminutive of all chameleons, ranging in size from 110mm to just 30mm. They are also almost totally terrestrial, spending the majority of their time on the forest floor. Only at night do some species climb up into the lower twigs of undergrowth to sleep. Their appearance reflects their preferred habitat – they are beautifully camouflaged when among leaves. Although the rainforests are their stronghold, certain *Brookesia* species are also found in some dry deciduous forest areas.

Though so tiny, and superficially so different from 'typical' chameleons, *Brookesia* share all the hallmark chameleon characteristics, although some of these are reduced: their ability to change colour is limited and their tail is short and only partially prehensile.

A common trait amongst the stump-tailed chameleons is to feign death if threatened. Some individuals fold their legs underneath their bellies and roll on to their side to resemble a dead leaf. Others flatten themselves laterally and produce rapid body vibrations to try and deter a would-be attacker. As a group, they are clearly successful: 26 *Brookesia* species are currently known and new ones are still being found.

Brookesia thieli

Brookesia decaryi

MB

Brookesia perarmata

MB

Brookesia superciliaris

MB

85

GECKOS: FAMILY GEKKONIDAE

In terms of species richness, geckos are amongst the most successful of all lizards, with about 1,000 species known worldwide; in Madagascar geckos outnumber all other lizard groups. The majority of geckos have specialised scales on their feet with microscopic hooks which allow them to cling to vertical surfaces. In most species the large eyes are protected by single transparent scales which are periodically licked clean by the gecko's long, flattened tongue.

They are generally nocturnal and brown in colour, but day geckos (genus *Phelsuma*) have been described as the 'living jewels of Madagascar' and have radiated into numerous flamboyant and beautiful species. The majority are emerald green with a variety of red, orange, blue or dark spots and blotches on their head, back and flanks. The largest is *Phelsuma madagascariensis grandis* (*left*) which reaches 30cm or more.

The big-headed geckos live on the ground and at night can be heard rustling around in the leaf-litter. There are 13 species on the island, widely distributed around the various types of forest. Those from the west and south, such as *Paroedura picta* (opposite) and *P. bastardi*, are the most likely to be seen. *P. masobe*, the largest of the genus and said to be the most beautiful, was only discovered in 1994 in low elevation rainforest.

Above Fish-scaled gecko (*Geckolepis typica*). These lizards are easily identified by their very large overlapping scales. Their response to predators is startling. If seized, they can shed their entire coat of scales in an instant, exposing the bare skin underneath, and make good their escape. The flayed gecko is a horrendous sight but the scales soon regenerate.

Below Big-headed gecko (*Paroedura picta*). These nocturnal geckos can be heard moving around in leaf-litter in many dry forest areas, such as Ampijoroa, Ankarana, Kirindy and Berenty.

AA

The Remarkable Uroplatus

The leaf-tailed or fringed geckos (genus *Uroplatus*) are amongst Madagascar's most extraordinary animals, demonstrating a superb mastery of camouflage. The largest species, *Uroplatus fimbriatus* (shown on the left and on page 131), perhaps illustrates this best. The skin colour and pattern exactly mimics its favoured tree trunk. The gecko rests motionless, head downward, stretching out its legs and spatula-like tail and flattening itself against the bark. A frill of skin around the lower part of the animal forms a continuous skirt which blends the outline of the gecko imperceptibly into the tree. To enhance the effect, these geckos can also change colour should they find themselves on a lighter or darker tree.

If this camouflage fails, *Uroplatus fimbriatus* has one more remarkable defensive trick up its sleeve. When alarmed it flicks its tail upwards, throws back its head and opens its mouth as wide as possible, showing a brilliant orange-red interior (see front cover). Another species, *U. henkeli*, adds a startlingly loud distress call to the gaping mouth threat.

At present 11 species are recognised, from the largest, *U. fimbriatus*, which can measure 30cm (and is best seen on Nosy Mangabe) to the smallest, *U. ebenaui*, which is about 7–8cm long. They are more abundant in rainforests, but are also found in deciduous forest. The larger species (see page 89) tend to mimic tree bark while the smaller ones (see page 90) look like dry leaves.

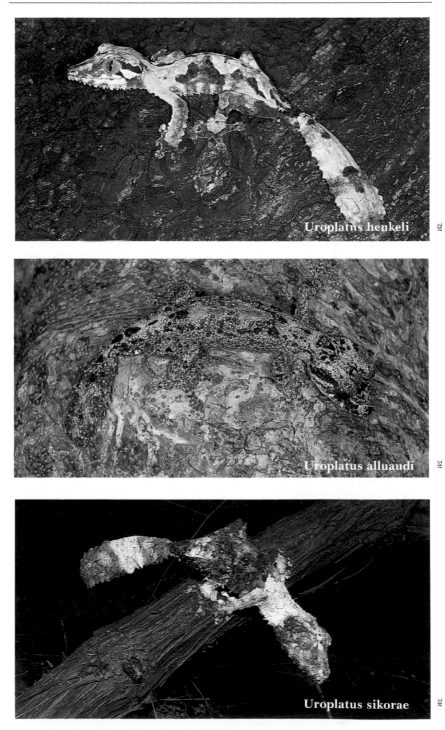

Uroplatus henkeli

Uroplatus alluaudi

Uroplatus sikorae

MB

Uroplatus lineatus

WL

Uroplatus phantasticus

NG

Uroplatus ebenaui

90

OTHER LIZARDS
Besides the chameleons and geckos, Madagascar is home to three other lizard families: the iguanids, plated lizards and skinks.

Iguanids: Family Iguanidae
As has already been mentioned, the presence of iguanids presents something of a riddle, as the stronghold of this group of lizards is Central and South America. In Madagascar they mainly inhabit the west and southwest of the island where the climate is hot and dry. The small, three-eyed lizard (*Chalaradon madagascariensis*) is particularly common in the dry south and in the spiny forest. Its 'third eye' is a pineal eye which shows as a conspicuous black dot on the back of its head. This 'eye' is found in many lizards and in some species is sensitive to light, possibly measuring periods of day and night.

The spiny-tailed iguanids, genus *Oplurus*, are common in the dry south and west of Madagascar. Their tails, which look like elongated fir cones, are used as a defensive barrier to their hiding places. These large lizards spend the day on rocks and trees, waiting for an insect meal to walk past. They also eat fruit and leaves.

Below Collared iguanid (*Oplurus cuvieri*). Normally these large lizards seem quite placid and are easy to approach. The skirmish here is probably over territory.

GT

Plated (Girdle-tailed) Lizards and Skinks:
Families Gerrhosauridae and Scincidae

The smooth, streamlined lizards belonging to these two families are sometimes mistaken for snakes as they move through the leaf-litter. Some species of skink add to this impression by having only vestigial legs.

Plated lizards are common throughout Madagascar. There are 13 species of *Zonosaurus*, all of which are found on the forest floor where they can be heard scurrying through the leaves.

Skinks are a familiar and large family of lizards (more than 1,200 species worldwide) but are perhaps the least studied of Madagascar's reptiles. Around 50 species are currently recognised. Many skinks have small limbs, and the near-limbless lizard, *Androngo* genus, has almost dispensed with them altogether. These burrowing skinks are sometimes seen at Berenty and on Nosy Mangabe.

Above Plated lizard (*Zonosaurus laticaudatus*). This lizard was photographed at Ampijoroa, but the species is widespread throughout Madagascar.

Below An unidentified *Amphiglossus* species from Ranomafana. Like *Amphiglossus astrolabi*, this large skink is unusual because of its aquatic habits – it is often found in streams.

SNAKES

Above One of 85 species of snake found in Madagascar. This is a recently described one, *Stenophis citrinus*, known from only a few specimens, and first collected in the forest of Beroboka in the southwest. There are many snakes in this genus awaiting formal identification.

Left Unidentified species. Probably undescribed!

The Boas: Family Boidae

Boas are primarily a South American group of snakes, though also found on Madagascar. There are three species, all of which show very close links to the boa constrictor from Central and South America.

The largest is the Madagascar ground boa (*Acrantophis madagascariensis*), which averages just under 2m in length but can reach 3m. Its geometric pattern of browns, creams, greys and black, helps the snake blend into the leaf-litter (see page 130). The ground boa hunts mainly at night and is particularly fond of small mammals (including lemurs). In the drier western forests, this species may, like some other snakes, spend the day in the underground burrows of ant colonies. Dumeril's boa (*Acrantophis dumerili*) is a closely related species from the south.

The Madagascar tree boa (*Sanzinia madagascariensis*) is the smallest and most common of the family. There is considerable variation in colour between snakes from different areas: those from the east sport a crazy-paving pattern of olive-green, grey and black, whereas those from western areas are much more brown. The juveniles are also a totally different colour (see below).

Left Madagascar tree boa (*Sanzinia madagascariensis*). Despite its name, it is often found on the ground. Much darker specimens are sometimes seen, with an almost iridescent blue sheen. A row of heat sensitive pits around their upper and lower lips helps it to find warm-blooded prey.

Below A juvenile of the same species. Its brilliant red colour will change to green as it matures.

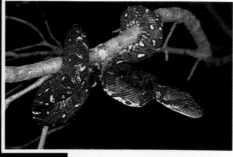

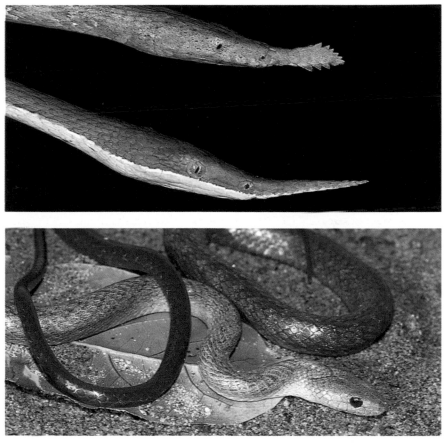

Above The spear-nosed snake (*Langaha madagascariensis*) is an excessively weird sight in an island full of such surprises. Both males and females have quite extraordinary noses. The two-tone male has a nose like a bayonet, whilst the female, which is disguised effectively as a twig, has a nose like a thorny club. This genus contains two other equally bizarre species, *L. alluaudi* (see page 131) and *L. pseudoalluaudi*.

Below The 'fandrefiala' (*Ithycyphus perineti*). Though harmless, this arboreal snake is much feared by some rural Malagasy. They believe it can mesmerise people or cattle passing below, then stiffen its body to drop like a spear, tail first, to impale the unfortunate victim. The blood-red body and tail would help create such a myth.

Family Colubridae

The vast majority of other snakes inhabiting Madagascar belong to the family Colubridae – commonly known as 'typical' snakes.

Quite frequently seen by visitors are the hog-nosed snakes (genus *Leioheterodon*). The largest of the three species, *Leioheterodon madagascariensis*, is reasonably common in rainforests but more likely to be seen in dry forests. It is a handsome yellow and black snake, which can reach a length of 150cm.

TORTOISES AND TURTLES: FAMILY TESTUDINIDAE

Madagascar has the unfortunate distinction of being home to some of the rarest tortoises in the world. Four species are endemic to the island. The largest is the plowshare tortoise or angonoka, *Geochelone yniphora*. Although now restricted to a tiny area around Soalala, west of Mahajanga, there is a successful breeding programme at Ampijoroa where around 300 angonoka have been successfully raised (2001).

The species gets its name from the long, upturned projection that extends from the plastron (lower shell). Males use this 'plowshare' to joust, trying to lever their opponents on to their backs and gain the attentions of onlooking females. In an unusually robust form of foreplay, they may also use it to roll the female over several times before mating.

Below: Plowshare tortoise (*Geochelone yniphora*)

The radiated tortoise (*Geochelone radiata*), found in the south and southwest, gets its name from the radiating patterns on its shell. The remaining two tortoise species are very much smaller. The dry deciduous forests around Morondava are the only known locality of the flat-tailed tortoise or kapidolo (*Pyxis planicauda*). The extreme climatic conditions of this area force them to aestivate during the dry season, burying themselves under leaf-litter and sand on the forest floor. Only after substantial rain do they become active. The spider tortoise (*Pyxis arachnoids*) has a much wider range and actually prefers the very dry conditions of the spiny forest areas. Both these species lay a single large egg, producing up to three eggs per season.

Of the four turtles, only one is endemic. The Madagascar big-headed, or side-necked, turtle (*Erymnochelys madagascariensis*), is found in western lakes and waterways. Its nearest relatives are in South America. This protected species has the unfortunate characteristic of growing to an edible size long before reaching sexual maturity, so may end up in the cooking pot before having the chance to reproduce. A breeding programme has been established at Ampijoroa.

Left Flat-tailed tortoise or kapidolo (*Pyxis planicauda*). Kirindy (in the wet season) is the best place to see it.

Below left Madagascar radiated tortoise (*Geochelone radiata*). Formerly abundant, its numbers have been reduced in recent years.

Below right The tortoises of the southwest, though officially protected, often fall prey to protein-hungry local people

FROGS

B ecause of their permeable skins amphibians cannot survive in salt water, so once Madagascar broke away from Africa those already in residence were marooned. Today, the only amphibians which survive on the island are frogs: there are no newts or salamanders. In splendid isolation these frogs have diversified into the present count of 220 species, although the true figure may be nearer 300. New ones are being discovered all the time: in the past five years at least 15 new ones have been described. Only a handful of families are represented (there are no toads, for instance) but some of these show enormous diversity. Ninety-nine percent of Madagascar's frogs are endemic.

TO FLAUNT OR TO CONCEAL?

The brightly coloured *Mantella* and well-camouflaged *Mantidactylus* genera form a subfamily, Mantellinae, belonging to the 'true frogs' (family Ranidae).

Mantellas show close similarities with the poison arrow frogs (Dendrobatidae) from South America, their colours warning predators to keep away. Their skin secretions are toxic, making them unpalatable. Confident in this protection, they are active by day; most frogs are nocturnal.

In contrast to the gaudy mantellas are the cryptically coloured *Mantidactylus* species. Perhaps none illustrates the art of camouflage better than *Mantidactylus aglavei* or uroplatus frog. Like the leaf-tailed gecko, it exactly matches its preferred resting place – in this case a mossy branch. In conjunction with its colour, frilly projections around its legs complete the disguise.

Above Mantidactylus pulcher. These little frogs live only on *Pandanus* palms, concealed by their green colour.

NG

NG

MB

Top Painted mantella (*Mantella madagascariensis*). This colourful species is quite common in the rainforest. During the breeding season they gather in their hundreds by streams and small pools.

Centre Golden mantella (*Mantella aurantica*). This tiny frog is only known from areas near Andasibe (Périnet).

Left Green-backed mantella (*Mantella laevigata*) lays its eggs in rainwater that has collected in tree holes. The South American poison arrow frogs do the same.

TREE FROGS

Generally speaking, tree frogs have enlarged fingertips to help them grip leaves, and big eyes for night vision. They are usually very photogenic, but to find them you must be prepared to spend many hours at night in the rainforest, systematically homing in on their calls. Rainy nights are the most productive.

One genus to look out for is *Heterixalus* which contains nine species. Most are green or yellow and several are distinctive in having conspicuous stripes running down their flanks. A notable exception is *H. alboguttatus*, one of the larger species (3cm) sometimes seen at Ranomafana. Its basic colour is blue/black with orange spots. However, in sunlight the blue deepens, the spots turn yellow and are ringed in black, while the underside of the hands and feet turn orange.

The 50 known species of *Boophis* are mainly tree frogs which breed in fast-moving streams. Although some are quite drably coloured, many are bright green or rich brown, and they have the most amazingly beautiful eyes! In some species the young change from green to brown as they mature. *Boophis madagascariensis*, for instance, is pale green with black and white markings as a froglet, but matures into a large brown frog that mimics leaf-litter. Its camouflage is enhanced by leaf-like projections from its knees, heels and elbows which break up its outline.

Below left Giant or white-lipped tree frog (*Boophis albilabris*). For a tree frog this is indeed a giant, reaching nearly 10cm in length. Note the well-developed webbing on the hands and feet. It is found near streams in montane rainforest, including Ranomafana.

Below right Boophis difficilis. This little tree frog (about 3cm long) is fairly common in the Andasibe (Périnet) area, where males call at night from vegetation 1–2m from the ground. The species name could derive from the frustrations of the taxonomist who finally sorted it out from a host of similar-looking little brown frogs!

MB

MB

Left A pair of *Mantidactylus boulengeri* and eggs. The eggs are laid on the forest floor. When the tadpoles hatch they wiggle their way to the nearest water to complete their lifecycle.

Some frogs have skipped the free-swimming tadpole stage altogether. Those in the genus *Stumpffia* lay their eggs in foam nests on the forest floor. The tadpoles develop into tiny froglets (only 3mm long) within this foam, eating nothing during the metamorphosis.

Left The tomato frog (*Dyscophus antongili*), is aptly named: that's just what it looks like in colour, shape and size! Apart from a few locations near Toamasina (Tamatave) the tomato frog is only known from the area around the Bay of Antongil (Masoala Peninsula) and the town of Maroansetra. Red means danger in the animal world, and if attacked this frog exudes a sticky white fluid which is toxic and, furthermore, gums up the predator's mouth.

Left Not many frog species inhabit the low rainfall areas such as the highlands and the southwest of Madagascar. One exception is *Scaphiophryne gottlebei*, a bizarre frog from Isalo National Park. During the prolonged dry season, it probably conceals itself underground and is only active after heavy rain. This frog was first described in 1992.

Left This pretty little tree frog, *Heterixalus madagascariensis*, is found in areas of high rainfall along the east coast. They can tolerate degraded habitat, so are relatively common. Tree frogs are easiest to spot at night, when they are most active, with the aid of a flashlight.

The Malagasy and their Environment

Madagascar annually goes up in flames. Over the centuries the forest that covered much of the island when the first people arrived some 2,000 years ago has been destroyed to make way for the crops and cattle on which the people survive. Folk memories of the great fires that raged across the island about a thousand years ago persist to this day.

For its size Madagascar is not overpopulated. In 2000 about 15 million people lived on an island more than twice the size of Great Britain: a population density of 21 people per square kilometre compared with 228 in Britain. But in 35 years Madagascar's population has doubled and its forest area has halved. Now only about 10% of the original forest remains, and the fertile soil is gone. Much of the once forested highlands are a barren wasteland where nothing will grow. The dry deciduous forests of the west, more vulnerable to fire than the rain-soaked east, are fast disappearing. And in 20 years there will be another 12 million people to feed.

Destruction of habitat is the main threat to Madagascar's wildlife, not hunting. Wild (and endangered) animals are still eaten, but taboos (*fady*) prohibit the killing of many species. As traditional beliefs break down, however, the wildlife is put further at risk. Madagascar's future is in the hands of the Malagasy. But to a hungry man it is the present that matters, not the future.

INVERTEBRATES

6 TO 600 LEGS

Invertebrates (animals without backbones) comprise over 95% of all animal species on earth. Since the break-up of Gondwanaland a myriad of invertebrates have evolved on Madagascar – no one yet knows just how many there are, but it is probably well over 100,000 species. It is beyond the scope of this book to do more than point out some of the most beautiful, colourful or extraordinary of these 'bizarre and wonderful forms'.

An observant visitor will notice an amazing number of these animals in Madagascar's forests. It is always worth turning over stones and logs (though be careful of scorpions), looking carefully on the underside of leaves and examining tree trunks for well-camouflaged invertebrates.

Absent insects are almost as interesting to entomologists as present ones. For example, there are no doryline ants (driver ants) and no large-mound, fungus-growing termites as seen in Africa (Macrotermitinae). Madagascar's termites create small mounds which are a distinctive aspect of the southern landscape. With this food source being relatively scarce, there are no mammals which feed exclusively on ants or termites.

Below left Shield bug (order Hemiptera, family Pentatomidae). Some of Madagascar's 200 or so species are quite large and gorgeously coloured, so are easy to see.

Below right Jewel beetle (order Coleoptera, family Buprestidae). There may be about 20,000 species of beetles in Madagascar, most of which are endemic. The underside of this jewel beetle almost glows with colour.

It is worth spending some time watching insect activity in Madagascar. At Berenty and Ampijoroa, for instance, you will see funnel-shaped holes in the sandy paths. These belong to ant-lion nymphs (order Neuroptera). If you are unkind enough to drop an ant into one of these, the 'lion' lurking below will pounce in a flurry of sand and grab the hapless insect.

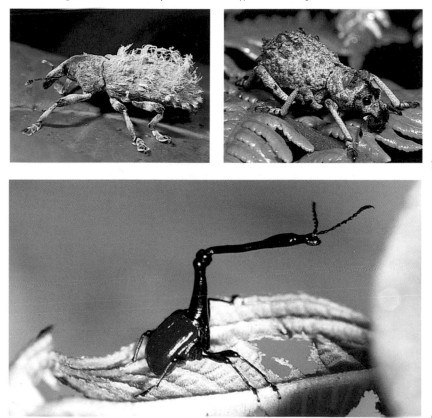

Weevils (order Coleoptera, family Curculionidae).
The countless weevil species (well over 1,000) come in many strange forms and colours.

Above left Lixus barbiger, from the eastern rainforest.

Above right Unidentified weevil from Mantadia National Park.

Below Giraffe-necked weevil (*Trachelophorus giraffa*). These extraordinary weevils are invariably found on the leaves of *Dichaetanthera Cordifolia* on which it feeds. The male's long 'neck' is adapted for rolling a leaf to make an egg case in which the female (which has a shorter neck) lays a single egg. They are very easy to see at Ranomafana, and to a lesser extent at Andasibe (Périnet).

A few of Madagascar's colourful or intriguing insects – and one mite (eight legs, not six).

Top left Giant katydid (family Tettigoniidae).
Centre left Shieldbug (family Scutellariidae).
Below left Cicada emerging from nymph.

Top right Lubber grasshopper (*Phymateus saxosus*).
Centre right Pentatomid bug.
Below right Giant red velvet mite
(*Dinothrombium pandorae*).

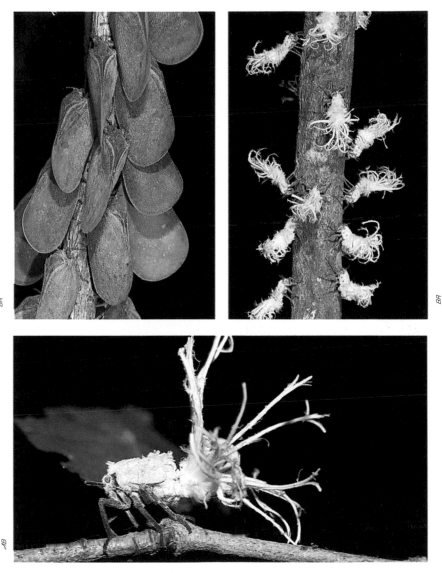

Flatid leaf-bugs. These remarkable bugs (*Phromnia rosea*) are quite easy to see in the wet season. The adults (*above left*) look like pink flowers (and a green form looks just like leaves). The nymphs (*above right and below*) excrete a sort of white waxy substance which 'grows' from the animal like long wispy feathers. If a bird or other predator makes a grab for one of these insects it gets a beakful of white nothing, and the animal hops away (this alone would be sufficient to protect it – it is almost as athletic as a flea). These bugs may be seen at Berenty, but a much bigger and more impressive form is found in the western forests.

The nymphs also excrete a sugary substance which solidifies in lumps on leaves in the forest; this candy treat is eaten by mouse lemurs, especially during the dry season.

NG

Above Male hissing cockroach (genus *Gromphadorrhina*). Even the cockroaches in Madagascar are appealing! Although very large (around 7cm) they are relatively slow-moving and very handsome. If prodded, males in particular emit a loud hiss which both deters predators (presumably) and is used to settle territorial disputes. Hissing cockroaches are easily found on night walks at Berenty where the lighter-coloured genus *Elliptorhina* can be seen waving their antennae out of holes in tree trunks.

QB

Above Scorpion (*Grosphus palpator*). For visitors, scorpions are effectively the only dangerous animals in Madagascar. They are active after rain and at night. During the day they like to hide under stones or in crevasses: beware! Boots or rucksack pockets are favoured places. The sting of the larger species from the western forests is excruciatingly painful to adults and can kill a child.

Millipedes.
Unlike centipedes which bite painfully, millipedes are harmless and attractive.
Above and centre The pill millipede (genus *Sphaerotherium*) comes in a variety of colours including green, and rolls itself into an impregnable ball when threatened.

Above The handsome giant millipede can exceed 15cm in length. Its many legs (over a hundred but not a thousand, as the name implies) enable it to cover all sorts of terrain – including vertical climbs – at a steady pace. The red colour warns potential predators that it is foul tasting. Nevertheless, lemurs have been known to eat them, wiping off the secretions on their tails!

The Orchid and the Moth

The delicately perfumed, white *Angraecum* orchids of Madagascar are one of the botanical delights of the island. The most famous is the comet orchid (*Angraecum sesquipedale*).

Some of the British missionaries who worked in Madagascar in the 19th century found the study and recording of the island's natural history a fascinating diversion, especially while travelling through the eastern rainforests en route to the capital from the port of Tamatave. The Reverend William Ellis described the comet orchid in his book *Three Visits to Madagascar during the Years 1853-1854-1856*, published in 1859. He later introduced it into Britain where James Bateman, a well-known horticulturist, cultivated it. Mr Bateman sent Charles Darwin some specimens.

In the second edition of his book *The Various Contrivances by which Orchids are Fertilised by Insects* (1904) Darwin wrote: 'The *Angraecum sesquipedale*, of which the large six-rayed flowers, like stars formed of snow-white wax, have excited the admiration of travellers in Madagascar, must not be passed over. A green, whip like nectary of astonishing length hangs down beneath the labellum. In several flowers sent to me by Mr Bateman I found nectarines eleven and a half inches

long, with only the lower inch and a half filled with nectar. What can be the use, it may be asked, of a nectary of such disproportionate length? We shall, I think, see that the fertilisation of the plant depends on this length, and on nectar being contained only within the lower and attenuated extremity. It is, however, surprising that any insect should be able to reach the nectar. Our English sphinxes have proboscides as long as their bodies; but in Madagascar there must be proboscides capable of extension to a length of between ten and eleven inches! This belief of mine has been ridiculed by some entomologists, but we now know from Fritz Muller that there is a sphinx moth in South Brazil which has a proboscis of nearly sufficient length...'

Within a year, a moth with a proboscis of 30cm (12 inches) was found in Madagascar! It was named *Xanthopan morgani praedicta* in honour of Charles Darwin's prediction.

BUTTERFLIES
AD MOTHS

Amarillae

LAND AND AIR PASSENGERS

Madagascar has around 4,000 species of moth and some 300 butterflies. Moths started to evolve long before butterflies and were undoubtedly part of the fauna of Gondwanaland; butterflies, on the other hand, are more likely to have been dispersed to the island. It is not surprising, therefore, that most families show affinities with African counterparts, but there are some links with India, other parts of Asia and South America. One of the puzzles is the apparent absence, for instance, of primitive moths such as the Hepialidae family.

There are some surprising absences. The lycaenids (lipenines) of Africa, which feed on lichen, do not occur in Madagascar; their niche is filled with the 300 or so species of footman moths (Lithosiinae).

Overleaf (page 111) This tiger moth has just emerged from its chrysalis under a strangler fig, the caterpillar's favourite food. When under threat the moth excretes a frothy substance, pyrazine, which smells strongly of crushed runner-beans. This warns potential predators that the insect is unpalatable. There is a closely related group of moths in South America which also feed on figs.

Below Cyligramma disturbans (family Noctuidae). This beautiful moth inhabits dark places such as caves and the understorey of the rainforest. The Malagasy believe them to be the embodiment of their ancestors and it is 'fady' (taboo) to kill them.

Above left The Urania moth (*Chrysiridia rhipheus*). At first glance this diurnal moth looks like a butterfly. It is closely related to the genus *Urania* which occurs in South America where it also feeds on Euphorbiaceae plants (genus *Omphalea*). One species of *Chrysiridia* also occurs in Tanzania.

Above right Madagascar's largest butterfly, *Atrophaneura anterior*. This swallowtail is a lepidopterological mystery. It appears to be close to the ancestral stock of birdwing butterflies (which occur in Southeast Asia) which poses the question: how did it reach Madagascar? (Butterflies are thought to have evolved after the breakup of Gondwanaland.)

Below The citrus swallowtail (*Papilio demodocus*). This is an African species whose caterpillars feed on the leaves of citrus trees. There are, however, three endemic species which are restricted to the western forests.

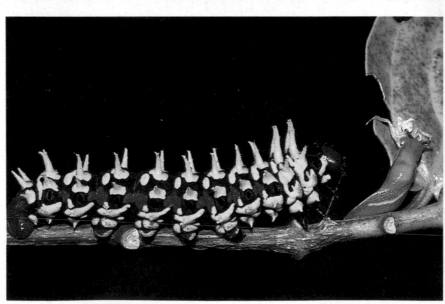

Above Comet moth (*Argema mittrei*). These handsome moths, whose caterpillars spin equally beautiful silvery cocoons, are much bigger (by a third) than their African relatives. They are bred commercially in Madagascar for collectors.

Below Caterpillar of the endemic emperor moth, genus *Maltagorea*, of the family Saturniiolae (the same as the comet moth), feeding on tapia in southern Madagascar.

SPIDERS

Nephila madagascariensis

SEX AND THE SINGLE SPIDER

Like all animals, spiders have two major preoccupations: food and sex. However, even a superficial study of the male spider's life (and death) will show that there is little pleasure in the latter. These two drives, eating and reproduction, are in uneasy conflict. Webs are designed to catch insects, and they are made by female spiders. This poses a problem for the male who has to trespass across her dinner table to pair up – she may mistake him for a meal. Since the male spider is often much smaller than the female this confusion is understandable, and he has to go to considerable efforts to achieve his goal without being eaten. His passionless sexual act begins with the depositing of sperm into a tiny homemade silk envelope before transferring the precious fluid into the hollow interior of a specially adapted leg called a pedipalp. Then comes the tricky part – getting it inside the female. Sometimes he taps out a code on the web to announce his presence, or presents the female with a tasty morsel to distract her. Alternatively, like the male golden orb-web spider, he may be so tiny he is not worth bothering about (see *opposite below*).

Wicked Wives but Marvellous Mums

Following mating the female is transformed into the perfect caring mother. She lays her eggs (many thousand, in some species) on a soft bed of silk which is delicately wrapped into a protective case or cocoon. Depending on the species, this is then either guarded in the web, hidden, or, as with wolf spiders, attached to the spinnerets and dragged about. When the tiny wolf spiderlings hatch they are carried about on their mother's back. During this long period of maternal care, the female does not eat.

Right A female wolf spider (family Lycosidae) with her brood. The female's back is covered with special stiff, knobbled hairs which the babies can hold on to.

Opposite above Golden orb-web spider. The yellow webs of *Nephila madagascariensis*, stretched between the telegraph wires, are an unmissable feature of many Malagasy towns and one that sets arachnophobes atremble. The silk of these webs is as tough as nylon, and indeed a textile industry using spider silk was attempted towards the end of the 19th century.

Opposite below The male *Nephila* is perched on the female's head and safely out of the way of her mighty jaws. If his pedipalp is loaded he can achieve the sexual act whenever he feels like it: she probably won't even notice!

NG

SG

NG

BR

Above Green lynx spider (*Peucetia madagascariensis*), an endemic species found in the eastern forests.

Right Argiope coquereli, an endemic species common in the western forests. The conspicuous zig-zag line of web is a strengthening structure called a stabilimentum; it may also attract insects to the web, rather as a bright-coloured flower might.

JH

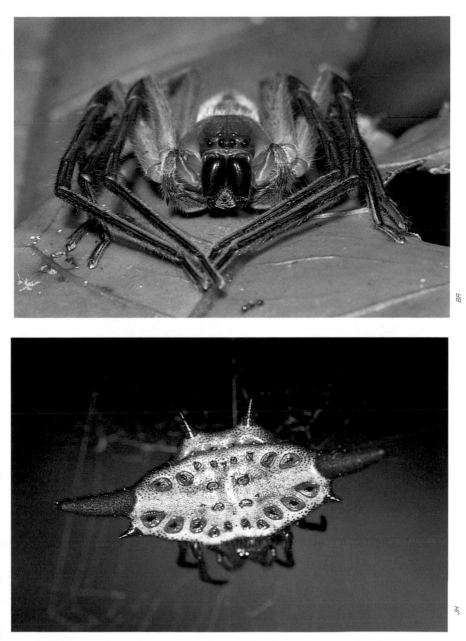

BR

JH

Above Unidentified huntsman spider. As the name implies, these spiders do not use webs to snare their prey, but chase and catch it instead. They have excellent eyesight.

Below Thorn spider, subfamily Gasteracanthinae. The thorn spider group is well known in Africa but has an endemic subspecies in Madagascar.

WL

Above Net-throwing spider (family Dinopidae). This is a widespread family of spiders with an extraordinarily elaborate – and effective – method of catching their prey. The spider first weaves a rectangular web of various types of silk, most of which are highly elastic. When this 'net' is finished, the spider grasps each corner in its four front legs, cuts the web free from its supports, and hangs head downward with the net at the ready. If an insect passes by, either on the wing or on foot, the spider lunges at it like a butterfly collector, the net being stretchy enough to enmesh even quite large prey.

SQUASHY THINGS

An aptly-named slug or nettle caterpillar of the Limacodidae family. The sharp scoli on their backs can deliver a painful sting.

SLUGS AND SNAILS, WORMS AND LEECHES

Few visitors are able to enthuse about the island's squashy things, but even these are often remarkable looking and have strange lifestyles. They are most commonly encountered after rain. Dry conditions force them to retreat to moist hiding places to avoid dehydration.

Madagascar's snails are of great interest to naturalists because there are so many species – probably close to 400 – and most are endemic. The introduced African giant landsnails (see page 122) indirectly nearly caused the extinction of many of these native species. In 1962 the *Euglandina* snail, a ferocious predator, was introduced into Madagascar in an irresponsible attempt to control the African intruder. Fortunately it did not survive. The introduced *Euglandina* has been responsible for the extinction of all endemic snails in the island of Moorea, in the South Pacific.

In addition to the flat worms and leeches, Madagascar has some impressively large earthworms, some nearly 30cm long. These inhabit the eastern rainforests and are a favourite food of tenrecs.

Above Giant landsnails mating. These huge snails, whose shells litter some forest floors, were introduced from Africa.

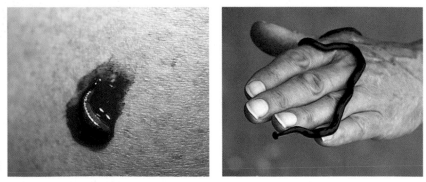

Above left Madagascar's leeches are small and do not live in water but hang around on bushes waiting for a host – usually a tourist – to walk past. They attach themselves to their victim with a tail-end sucker and inject an anticoagulant into the wound made with their sharp jaws. The bite is painless but the result is messy. Once the leech has had its fill it falls off, but the bitten area can itch for several days. Leeches are mostly gut: pouches all down the digestive tract enable the animal to hold a large quantity of blood. A satiated leech is about four times its hungry size. At least it does not need to feed again for several months – the time it takes to digest this banquet of blood.

Above right This impressive animal is not a leech but a flatworm. Madagascar has several species, many of which are brightly coloured with two-tone stripes running down their bodies. All have hammer-shaped heads and are harmless.

MADAGASCAR AT NIGHT

Madagascar scops owl *(Otus rutilus)*

FROM DUSK TO DAWN

One of the joys of walking in a Malagasy forest is the safety. There are no large animals hiding in the trees, no venomous snakes concealed in the foliage and almost no horrible creepy-crawlies lurking in the undergrowth (scorpions are the exception). To add to the excitement, the day and night shifts are completely different. Come dusk, when all the familiar daytime creatures are bedding themselves down, a new cast of characters is stirring. These include nocturnal lemurs, carnivores, nocturnal birds, *Uroplatus* geckos, frogs and a myriad of insects. These are Madagascar's spirits of the night.

Of course, the fundamental problem to seeing nocturnal animals is the dark. However, there are tell-tale signs to look for. The back of the eye (retina) in most nocturnal animals is highly reflective. This specialised area, the tapetum, increases the sensitivity of the eye to dim light. It also reflects incoming light straight back out again, so the eyes of an animal looking towards you appear to glow red or green in the torchlight. This is commonly called 'eyeshine'.

Above Brown mouse lemur (*Microcebus rufus*). Many of Madagascar's most interesting animals may only be seen at night. Guided night walks are available in many of the national parks and reserves and can be very rewarding (see page 126).

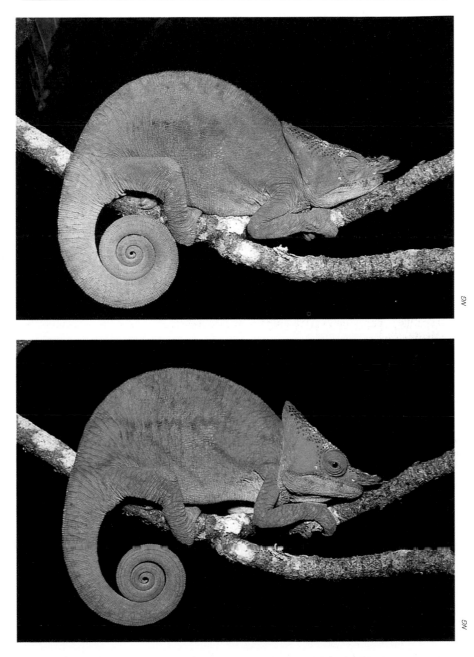

Above Chameleons are easier to see at night because they turn a much lighter shade; some species become almost white. The Parson's chameleon is in typical sleeping posture in the top picture: tail coiled, chin resting on the branch. Woken by the flash of the first photo, his skin has already darkened and his tail uncoils in preparation for a quick getaway.

125

A Shot in the Dark

Night-time wildlife watching (and photography) is not just a case of where to look but how to look. Here are some hints.

- Avoid times of the full moon. Many animals will be in hiding.
- Wear appropriate clothing: subdued colours and rustle-free fabrics.
- Bring binoculars. They are helpful even in torchlight.
- Use a head torch in conjunction with a powerful hand torch. Halogen bulbs are best. Bring plenty of new batteries and replacement bulbs.
- The first two hours after dark are best. Nocturnal animals have just woken up so are more active and often encountered. Later at night many go back to sleep again.

Now that you are ready, what do you look for? At first only use the head torch and set the beam focus so that it throws a fairly wide and diffuse pool of light. Then search the pool of light using your peripheral vision, that is, avoid looking directly at something of interest. In dim light you will actually see it more clearly out of the corner of your eye.

If something catches your attention – a pair of red glowing eyes, for instance – illuminate it fully with the hand torch and check it out using binoculars. Should the animal take flight, shut down the lights, wait and start again – it may resettle close by.

Here's where to look for your favourite creatures:

Lemurs The smaller species can be seen anywhere, but it is easiest to concentrate on the lower, thinner branches that they prefer. Lepilemurs and woolly lemurs are generally found clinging to narrower vertical trunks. Always investigate the areas around tree holes, especially at dusk when animals have just woken up.

Chameleons Often sleep at the ends of branches, and their night-time light colour stands out in a torch beam. Always check the lower branches around the outside of bushes and trees. Stump-tailed chameleons are found really low down or on the ground. It's just a question of grubbing about.

Uroplatus The larger species like *U. fimbriatus* hunt from ground level to the canopy. Their eyes do shine red, but not as brightly as those of lemurs, and you'll only see one eye at a time. The smaller species tend to be on finer branches of undergrowth and amongst leaves, so are much harder to find.

Frogs Many species tend to be very vocal at night, so are heard but not always seen. They often sound closer than they actually are.

Invertebrates Some also have eyeshine. Check the forest floor and tree bark for spiders, the ends of twigs where butterflies and moths sometimes roost, the underside of leaves for stick insects and mantids, and fallen trees and rotten logs for millipedes, beetles and bugs.

Birds Go out a couple of hours before dawn. You can then catch the nocturnal birds and be on the spot at daybreak when the diurnal species are at their most active.

CAMOUFLAGE

Collared nightjar *(Caprimulgus enarratus)*

SAFETY MATCHES

A lthough the number of true carnivores in Madagascar is relatively few (just eight), plenty of other species make their living eating other animals. Not surprisingly, as predators develop more efficient ways of hunting, prey endeavours to keep that half pace ahead. An obvious way to do this is to not be seen in the first place and an impressive array of animals have evolved spectacularly convincing camouflage.

The collared nightjar (see page 127) is a nocturnal bird that spends the day roosting amongst leaf-litter of the rainforest floor – something that makes it potentially vulnerable to predators. It has evolved intricately patterned plumage that exactly matches the background of dry leaves, moss and twigs, and like so many well-camouflaged animals they are able to keep remarkably still when danger is near, only taking flight when the threat gets uncomfortably close.

Cryptic colouration like that of nightjars or the Madagascar ground boa ensures that the animal blends with its background. Other animals take this a stage further, by evolving body parts or adornments that look just like elements of their habitat such as leaves, twigs, bark or even flower petals.

Opposite The Parson's chameleon and *Mantydactylus* frog are both examples of cryptic colouring. They blend with the greens and browns of their forest habitat.

Below Twig-mimic mantis. Many insect and some reptile species look like twigs, leaves, or moss. They do more than blend with the background – they become part of it.

NG

129

Top left Moss-mimic stick insect (*Parectatosoma macquesi*).

Top right Stick insect.

Above left Leaf-mimic mantis.

Above right Cryptically coloured ground boa (*Acrantophis madagascariensis*).

Top left Female twig-mimic snake
(*Langaha alluaudi*).

Top right Leaf-tailed gecko
(*Uroplatus finbriatus*).

Above Stump-tailed chameleon
(*Brookesia stumpffi*).

Right 'Lined' Leaf-tailed gecko
(*Uroplatus lineatus*).

Photography

Much of the wildlife in Madagascar is approachable. To take excellent photographs like those in this book you do not need very expensive equipment; the secret is getting into the right place at the right time and knowing what to do when you get there. Here are some hints:

• The camera body should have the option of a wide range of different lenses and other accessories, such as flashguns.

• Choose the best lens you can afford. The type of lens will be dictated by the subjects you most wish to photograph.

• 'Professional' quality film is worth the extra expense. Recommended is Fujicolour 100 for prints, with Fujichrome Velvia 50 and Fujichrome Provia 100 or Sensia 100 for transparencies.

• Whenever possible use a tripod with a cable release. Without a tripod a good rule of thumb is never use a shutter speed slower than the reciprocal of the focal length of the lens, ie: with a 50mm lens, 1/60th second, with 100–135mm lenses, 1/125th second.

• Consider the background to your photographs. Getting this right is often the difference between a mediocre and a memorable image.

• If it does not look good through the viewfinder, it will never look good as a picture. Be patient. Wait until the background is uncluttered and there is a natural highlight in the eyes. It makes all the difference.

Birds and Mammals

A lens of at least 300mm is necessary for bird photography to produce a reasonable image size. Optics of this length should always be held steady on a tripod. The subject needs to be well lit, but the majority of species in Madagascar are forest-dwellers; a powerful flashgun adds extra light to pep up the subject. For use with longer lenses a flash unit with a guide number of 30 or more is best. This will allow subjects over 10m away to be photographed, and the extra light can transform an otherwise dreary picture by 'lifting' the subject out of its surroundings and putting the all-important highlights into the eyes.

Small Things: Macro Photography

Macro lenses of around 50mm and 100mm cover most subjects and these create images up to half lifesize in the viewfinder. For further enlargement extension tubes will be required.

At distances of less than a metre, apertures as small as between f16 and f32 are necessary to ensure adequate depth of field, plus flash to provide enough light. Most manufacturers make macro-flash set ups including ring-flashes. These, however, tend to produce very 'flat' lighting that can make the subject look two-dimensional. A better solution is to build your own bracket and use one or two small flashguns to illuminate the subject from the side. The resulting shadows give the subject depth.

Further Reading

Travel and Other Natural History Guides

Madagascar: The Bradt Travel Guide. Hilary Bradt (1999, 6th ed.). Bradt Travel Guides. The best general guide to the country.

Globetrotter Travel Guide to Madagascar. Derek Schuurman and Nivo Ravelojaona (1997). Struik/New Holland. A travel guide aimed at the ecotourist.

Mammals of Madagascar. Nick Garbutt (1999). Pica Press. Fully comprehensive guide to the island's amazing mammals. Illustrated with the author's colour photographs and detailed ink drawings. Distribution maps and recommended viewing sites for all species.

Lemurs of Madagascar – A Tropical Fieldguide. Russell Mittermeier et al. (1994). Conservation International. A very good pocket reference to the island's endemic primates. Well illustrated with paintings.

The Birds of Madagascar – A Photographic Fieldguide. Pete Morris and Frank Hawkins (1998). Pica Press. A comprehensive and up-to-date review of the island's avifauna, covering all 280 species recorded on the island to date. Fully descriptive text and illustrated with 500 colour photographs.

Birds of the Indian Ocean Islands: Madagascar, Mauritius, Réunion, Rodrigues, Seychelles and the Comoros. Ian Sinclair and Olivier Langrand (1998). New Holland. A guide covering the 338 bird species from Madagascar and other Indian Ocean islands. The text is scant and sometimes inaccurate; the colour plates by several leading bird artists also vary in their accuracy.

A Fieldguide to the Amphibians and Reptiles of Madagascar. Frank Glaw and Miguel Vences (1994). A thorough look at the island's amazing herpetofauna. Well written and illustrated. Rather expensive but invaluable for those with a special interest in these animals.

Madagascar: A Natural History. Ken Preston-Mafham (1991). Facts on File. A large format general account of the island's wildlife, although some of it is now outdated. Beautifully illustrated with photographs.

Specialist Natural History

Lemurs of Madagascar: An Action Plan for their Conservation. Russell Mittermeier et al. (1992). The latest priorities for the conservation of lemurs.

Lemurs of Madagascar and the Comoros – IUCN Red Data Book. Caroline Harcourt and Jane Thornback (1990). IUCN – Cambridge and Switzerland. A scientific review of the conservation status of each lemur taxon.

The Primates of Madagascar. Ian Tattersall (1982). Columbia U.P. An academic account of the biology and evolutionary history of the lemurs.

A Guide to the Birds of Madagascar. Olivier Langrand (1990). Yale U.P. Because of its largish size, this can hardly be considered a fieldguide, however, it is comprehensive and worth considering for the keen birdwatcher. Let down by rather poor illustrations and now superseded to an extent by the two titles above.

Chameleons – Nature's Masters of Disguise. James Martin and Art Wolfe (1992). Blandford Press. A fully illustrated look at the world of the chameleon – includes accounts of many Malagasy species.

Madagascar: An Environmental Profile. Alison Jolly et al. (1984). Pergamon Press. A good basic reference, but much of the detail is now out of date.

Madagascar: Profile de l'environnement. M.D. Jenkins (ed.) (1990). IUCN/WWF. A review of the protected areas and wildlife. Rather specialist. Mainly in French.

Madagascar: Revue de la Conservation et des Aires Protégées. Martin Nicoll and Olivier Langrand (1989). WWF – Switzerland. A comprehensive review of all the island's protected areas and the species they contain. Rather specialist. Mainly in French.

Background Reading

The Aye-aye and I. Gerald Durrell (1992). Harper Collins. Gerald Durrell recounts what turned out to be his last collecting expedition to Madagascar.

Zoo Quest to Madagascar. David Attenborough (1961). Lutterworth. An early account of some of the first-ever filming trips to Madagascar.

Madagascar: A World Out of Time. Frans Lanting (1990). Hale. A stunning, sometimes surreal photographic essay of the people, wildlife and landscapes of Madagascar.

Lemurs of the Lost World. Jane Wilson (1990). Impact Books. A fascinating account of the author's expedition to the Ankarana caves in northern Madagascar.

Emerald plated lizard
(*Zonosaurus boettgeri*).

INDEX